WHO I AM

Spiritual growth is an ongoing journey of awakening and re-orienting oneself toward God.

Who I Am

JOANNE VERRILL

BEKKER MEDIA

Copyright © 2025 by Joanne Verrill
All rights reserved. No part of this book may be reproduced in any manner whatsoever without written permission except in the case of brief quotations embodied in critical articles and reviews.

First Printing, 2025
First published by Bekker Media, 2025

Scriptures marked NIV are taken from the NEW INTERNATIONAL VERSION (NIV): Scripture taken from THE HOLY BIBLE, NEW INTERNATIONAL VERSION ®. Copyright© 1973, 1978, 1984, 2011 by Biblica, Inc.™. Used by permission of Zondervan.

Scriptures marked NKJV are taken from the NEW KING JAMES VERSION (NKJV): Scripture taken from the NEW KING JAMES VERSION®. Copyright© 1982 by Thomas Nelson, Inc. Used by permission. All rights reserved.

Scriptures marked ESV are taken from the THE HOLY BIBLE, ENGLISH STANDARD VERSION (ESV): Scriptures taken from THE HOLY BIBLE, ENGLISH STANDARD VERSION ® Copyright© 2001 by Crossway, a publishing ministry of Good News Publishers. Used by permission.

Cover design by Joy Churchhill

A copy of this title is held at the National Library of Australia.

Dedication

You know that feeling when life throws you so many curveballs, you start wondering if the universe is trying to beat you at some cosmic game of dodgeball?

Navigating the twists of identity, faith, and friendship can be as tricky as assembling IKEA furniture without instructions—frustrating, confusing, but oddly rewarding once you get it right.

This is my real-life roadmap for anyone looking to find your footing, just a little less solo and a lot more connected.
This book is a thank-you letter to the mob of amazing, devoted people around me who have continued to champion me throughout my life. We are not designed to live solo lives, and without my family and my friends, I simply would not have found such purpose and belonging.

This book is inspired by the many young people whom I work with every day. The battle to find identity in our chaotic world can be overwhelming. If the telling of my story helps just one young person find their feet to move forward, then it has served its purpose.
And finally, this book is a result of my faith in God. Who I am is all because of who He is.

Contents

Dedication		v
	Introduction	1
1	Foundation	3
2	The Dream Of A Ten-Pound Pom	5
3	Marmalade Toast	19
4	New Home Life	21
5	And Then There Was One	25
6	Shadows	31
7	New Options	37
8	Woman At The Well	45
9	Weather Changes	51
10	Change And Adventure	59
11	The Back End Of Nowhere	67
12	Trust That The Storm Will Pass	71
13	Grow Where You're Planted	79
14	Giving Makes The Way	87
15	Working, It's What You're Good At	93
16	Help!	103
17	Turning Point	111
18	Understanding Comes After Commitment	121

19	So, Who Am I?	123
20	Did I Finish University?	125
21	Can These Dry Bones Live?	129

Acknowledgments   131

Introduction

To tell the story of who I am, I must share with you how I began - and continue - to discover who I am through the Great I Am. To be honest, I could probably condense the message of my life into a few short sentences: God is Holy. He is sovereign. He sees me, and He desires me to be in His presence. How I came to the understanding of who God is also demonstrates God's magnificent love, power, and grace.

Growing up in a chaotic and unpredictable home, established in me some rather uncomfortable thoughts of who I believed I was, which led to some very pressing questions spinning around in my head. I questioned the value of life. I questioned my gender identity. I also questioned whether others valued me.

The absence of any input from my parents meant that I had no one to hear my thoughts or to correct the conversations taking place in my mind. Like so many things, if left unchecked and ignored, the poisonous thoughts that send us spiralling can quickly lead us into a place of torment. These thoughts and ideas grafted themselves to my very identity and became like unwanted tumours leeching life from me.

The most remarkable thing is that a forgotten child is never forgotten by God.

God's will for us is that our minds are free from painful thoughts. The process of removing these harmful thoughts and renewing our minds and habits of thinking can be painful and uncomfortable, especially after building our beliefs and identity on these thoughts. Extracting them is never easy or pleasant, but absolutely necessary to live the life that we were built for.

This story will take you on a loop that shows how I came to ask these questions and we'll finish off where we started – the questions have answers which I now hold as strong convictions that connect me with purpose. I believe that by reading my story you, the reader, will come to a place of knowing God just a little bit more, just as I did. This will help you adjust your course - from wandering around in the wilderness or maybe cause you to question your thoughts and direction. I had to face all these questions head-on in order to find myself, to find my identity, and to find my purpose.

I've been a Christian for over thirty years, and I promise you it has been a process of redirecting my life away from the old and into the new. This process continues today. It's been a process of awakening and of finding myself in Him. But first, I had to discover who He is. The biggest question I had to answer was: Who is the Great I Am?

Chapter 1

Foundation

Our childhood always plays a major role in who we become as adults. We learn boundaries. We learn our worth. We learn how to respond to authority. We learn how to love and how to be loved. We learn how to resolve conflict, and we learn when to fight and how to walk away from the fight. All this learning usually happens in the governing institute we call the family. Mothers represent how a woman can be treated and how she should carry herself. Fathers can demonstrate how a man can act towards others, protect his family, and respond to all kinds of situations. Both figures are also the 'law of the land' within the home.

As children, we build our values and beliefs based on our relationship with our parents. As we grow and come of age, daring to venture into the world around us, we take all that we have learned, weaving it into our hearts until it becomes our very identity. This becomes our foundation and what we build our life upon. As we insert ourselves into the wider community, this foundation now affects and impacts every aspect of the world around us - how we relate to and value others, our work ethics, the way we value the environment, the way we steward our finances, and what we find fulfilment in.

What happens though, when the foundation of our life has been inaccurately built - when we have been taught the wrong way to respond to the world around us, or have maybe misinterpreted what we have been taught? Most parents raise their children with integrity, teaching them right from wrong. They want them to prosper in later years. But mistakes are made, which impact the development of a child. However, the trajectory of the child's life is not set in stone because, as adults, they now have the incredible freedom to choose whether to build upon damaging lessons from the past or to rebuild on the truth.

Chapter 2

The Dream Of A Ten-Pound Pom

My childhood was far from normal, and nowhere close to any form of typical. However, I'll start by saying I am truly thankful for every challenge, every moment of chaos, and every battle in my home, as it taught me something enormously powerful – how to walk through hell.

My mother and father were ten-pound-poms. They immigrated from England in the 1960's. This was a time when Australia was offering free immigration to skilled workers. The government covered the cost of moving and setting your life up in Australia for £10. If things didn't work out and you wished to return to your place of origin, you would be required to pay back the total cost of the trip. Sounds like a dream for many people wishing to start afresh in a new, exotic country. And let's be honest, what a bargain at just £10!

Mum and Dad could have chosen Canada or South Africa instead of Australia. Seriously. Thank God Australia was their chosen destination! No offence to any Canadians or South Africans out there. I've just become so thankful for my life in Australia that I can't imagine growing up and living in any other nation. My stomach does not have the digestive power to cope with the high intake of biltong, a mandated dietary requirement of South Africans. Also, I would have grown up in the apartheid era, and what a different world that would have been. My bones would have ceased to function in the chilly Canadian climate, reducing my existence to mainly indoor living, venturing into the wider population for only micro-dose moments.

So, my parents set off to seek new beginnings, possibly trying to escape the pain and hurt that they had both grown up with in England, and, no doubt, holding firm to the expectation of hope and success they had heard was waiting for them in the land down under.

Dad had started his working career as a firefighter and served his community well in his early twenties. He then established himself as a technical engineer, completing trade certificates and establishing a good, honest reputation in the field. Mum was also a professional woman; she gained a high level of secretarial skill in her early twenty's and was easily able to find work in Australia thanks to her efficiency and high standards within the workplace. When he applied for immigration, Dad had already secured a job as an engineer in the gas industry in Melbourne, Victoria. Dad was a man who didn't like to take risks. If change were to occur, he would do all he could to ensure the outcome was relatively risk-free.

When I look back at their humble beginnings, it's extremely hard to imagine these two people taking on such an adventure. Later in their lives, they avoided change at all costs. Neither of them spoke in depth about how they experienced the changes of moving to a new country. I can only suppose that it was terrifying, but the dream of the life they were planning to build energised them to take such a giant leap of faith.

Mum and Dad never really spoke of their childhood or went into detail about how they met, how they fell in love, or what the turmoil was like for them when things started to fall apart. But the few things I do know about their life before Australia has given me valuable insight into why things ended up the way they did.

Dad always spoke fondly of his mother and father, and older brother John (Jack). Sadly, though, Dad and Uncle Jack became orphans at an early age. Their father (and my paternal grandfather) passed away in 1943, serving as a serviceman for the Royal Merchant Navy in the Second World War. My grandfather served in both the First and Second World Wars. He worked on the supply ship transporting goods to the men and women on the front line. My dad was only one year old, and Uncle Jack was six at the time their father was killed. My grandma became a grieving wife and single mother of two small boys amidst a devastating time of war. With no government support, she had to work two jobs - cleaning during the day, and barmaid by night.

My dad recalled one or two stories of going with her to the cleaning jobs and entertaining himself while she worked. When Dad was of school age, he was sent to boarding school, as his father served in the Royal Merchant Navy, and education for children of servicemen and women was looked after by the armed forces. I could think of nothing worse than leaving my family and my home, to move to a regimented boarding school at such an early age. However, I think this environment gave my dad the structure and security that he needed. He only ever spoke highly of his time there, which I still find hard to believe. Because of the age difference, Dad and his brother had little to do with each other, and their relationship was never close.

The battling family was about to be struck with tragedy again when, at the tender age of ten, my father was called into his headmaster's office for a serious conversation. He was abruptly informed that his mother had died. With little understanding and no time to grieve or process this devastating news, Dad was sent back to his class to continue his day. Decades later, my uncle Jack decided to investigate their mother's death. As the boys were under the age of eighteen, they were never given a death certificate and never knew why or how their mother passed so suddenly. In his late sixties, Uncle Jack acquired the death certificate and discovered that their mother had 'died at the hands of another' during a backyard abortion. This news devastated both my father and uncle Jack as they suddenly learned that their mother's death was in fact, preventable, and they could have had another sibling. Their childhood could have been quite different. My father grieved the loss of his mother all over again, or maybe, receiving the death certificate, Dad was finally able to grieve for the first time. Uncle Jack was fifteen and left school to move home. They would have lost the family home if no one had occupied it. (Honestly, I don't think Uncle Jack cared much for school, so leaving early served him well. He later joined the Navy and had a colourful and fulfilling career, enjoying every moment of it.) This left my dad in a dank, loveless environment, with no one to nurture, care for, and protect him. Dad had no choice but to come to terms with now being alone in the world. They had only one other living relative that we know of - an older woman, called Aunt Maggie, who cared for Dad on school breaks.

Childhood for Dad was far from bliss, yet he never disregarded his childhood or felt spiteful about his circumstances. He was grateful for his education and the little kindness that was shown towards him at the boarding school. He was proud of both his parents and the sacrifices they had made. The effects of the loss of his mother took a massive toll on him; I believe Dad never recovered from that loss. Dad passed away recently, and his final wish was to have his ashes returned to the mother country, England, and have them spread on his mother's grave. I think part of this wish demonstrated his longing to be with his mother, and partly a stubborn Yorkshire man who loved his country dearly and had every intention of finishing his journey right back where he started.

Dad's parents, my grandparents, early 1930's

Mum's childhood story lacks detail. Well, to be frank, almost nothing is known about how she was raised. Her mother was strict and dominating, and her father was quietly spoken and designated to the background of family life. Mum found it hard to talk about what life was like for her growing up, which leaves me guessing as to what she might have experienced.

Mum had one younger sister, Aunty Yvonne, and stated that Yvonne was the obvious favourite. As a result, Mum wasn't treated well by her parents. However, she spoke fondly of her grandparents, whom she spent time with, and would go to church with them whenever she was with them. Due to my Mum's poor health later in life, I believe that what she experienced was damaging and never really dealt with, so, it was carried over into adulthood.

Mum and Dad met at a local dance. You know the type where young lasses and lads get together every Friday night to twirl, foxtrot, and jive the night away. (These are all dance moves for you, slightly uncultured readers.)

I sometimes wish I had grown up in that era when dances and community events filled the calendar. However, being left-handed, I don't believe the world was ready for my level of uncoordinated freestyle moves. In my mind, I would have been like Judy Garland... but, no, I would have been something else!

I never had the opportunity to hear from either Mum or Dad what the beginning of their relationship was like. Dad once explained to me that when he was at Mum's parents' house, you only spoke if you were spoken to. He also said that he never asked questions about her upbringing or gained any knowledge of her early childhood experiences, which seems crazy to me. I am always naturally curious and intrigued by other people's stories and experiences. I firmly believe that the more you understand a person, the less likely you are to react to their behaviour—and the more equipped you become to truly help and champion them. In any case, a thorough background check doesn't go astray.

Mum and Dad embarked on their immigration adventure in 1967. It was a three-month journey on a boat, crossing the ocean, stopping over in South Africa and other fascinating ports before they finally arrived in Melbourne. They moved into their new home in Mount Eliza, Victoria, and started working almost right away. Dad had his job lined up as an engineer for Global Mobile (an international gas company), and Mum continued her work as a secretary for the same company.

Neither Mum nor Dad spoke about their relationship during this time, except that they enjoyed exploring and establishing themselves as locals within their new surroundings. Dad always enjoyed speaking of how his career blossomed and his reputation grew in those years alongside a booming industry. I feel Dad's confidence within himself grew as his identity became entwined in his career.

From what I could gather, the desire for children was strong, but they were unable to get pregnant initially. Adoption was common in those days, so they went through the application process and waited to receive the call that would quickly launch them into parenthood. The call did come, they had been successful, and a newborn baby boy was about to enter their world. What a crazy thing to go through. No preparation, just twenty-four hours to adjust to your new life, and bam, you're a parent! My eldest brother was warmly welcomed into the Verrill home, and according to photo evidence, he was a sweet little poppet. I can only imagine how big of an adjustment this was for both Mum and Dad. A short time later, bam, mum was pregnant with my second eldest brother. It was never discussed why Mum and Dad struggled in the first place to become pregnant, but it seemed that taking the pressure off, or maybe the distraction of having a baby, helped them easily conceive their second child.

The boys were only eleven months apart, so they grew up close together. Mum's parents visited England after the boys turned one. There are many photos of family outings, trips to the beach, and camping at this stage of early parenthood and family life. Life seemed normal, but I do not doubt that raising two boys with no immediate family or close friends around would have been extremely challenging.

My sister was born two years later. (Sometimes telling my family's story is like piecing together an Agatha Christie novel, without the murder, of course. Or playing the role of "The Number One Lady Detective") Due to the lack of information supplied by my parents, I've become well-trained in looking for clues to tell their story. Fewer photos appearing in the albums, I believe, tell a story of darkness beginning to fall on our family. Mum's mental health began to show cracks, and in 1979, Mum was diagnosed with schizophrenia.

Dad told me an odd story of what life was like then, but the pain of retelling it was often too much for him. He described her 'episodes' as "out of control" and "violent". I believe Dad carried a lot of shame for how he may have reacted to the situation and how other people may have perceived the family. Dad once told me that one particular day Mum had kicked him out of the house; however, after leaving, he received a phone call from the police requesting him to return. It seemed that while Mum was experiencing psychosis, she had trashed the house and was not stable enough to be left alone with the children.

Dad and I, 1984.

Over the next decade, Mum's mental health became more and more unstable and put immense pressure on their marriage. The lack of understanding about this type of disorder, no close community around the young family, and Mum and Dad's very English culture - combined with their own painful experiences from the past - were all taking their toll. It gives me a heavy heart to think about what my older siblings would have seen and heard behind closed doors. In a way, because of the nine-to-eleven-year age gap, my siblings and I grew up in hugely different homes and even with quite different parents.

Dad's career, on the other hand, was taking off. Due to the demand within the oil and gas industry, he had established himself as a reputable engineer, so he was offered jobs across the country. Dad was offered a consulting engineering position through ESSO in their head office situated in Sale in Gippsland, Victoria. Mum and Dad chose to accept the opportunity and reset their lives in rural Victoria. The change in scenery sparked the return of some romance and passion in their marriage, as this is when I was conceived. Planned? Definitely not! I remember doing the maths when I was around seven years old, and realised there was a significant gap between myself and my siblings. I asked Dad if I was unplanned. His response was perfect. "You weren't planned; you were a wonderful surprise."

There is such power in our words, and how Dad responded to my question was so satisfying and, at that moment, I was content with my place in the family. I like to refer to this season in my parent's life as a "midlife special". At forty-one in the eighties, they were about to start again with a new baby, a new home in a new community, and with new hope.

Early memories for me were far from a regular family experience. In my memories, my mum's mental health was very fragile, and she was unable to nurture and care for her family, which I feel may have added to her anguish.

Memories of Mum were of her having manic episodes when she would experience debilitating depression, or she would be explosively angry. I was reluctant to invite friends over as she could ignite at any point, and I was understandably anxious about how others might be affected by her brokenness.

Personally, I never felt fearful of her or her behaviour. Maybe because that was all I knew; it was completely normal for me. We didn't grow up with extended family or knitted into a community, so I was never really exposed to other families in my early years, not until a few years into my schooling.

My siblings in their early years with Dad

When Mum was experiencing an episode, both she and Dad would have arguments that were loud and hurtful towards each other. It was always at night after I was in bed, because, of course, it was believed that children didn't hear arguments at night in their bedroom. These arguments would escalate, and all I remember is how they ended - out of hopelessness, anger and defeat Dad would yell at Mum, "Fine then, I'll leave and I'll fucking kill myself then!" I would hear those awful words, and absolute fear would grip me. Fear of Dad leaving and fear of him dying. Our family was in chaos, but Dad was trying his best to hold the ship on course. Without him, who would hold it all together?

Part of trying to help Mum and see her get better involved frequent trips to a psych ward. It is important to note here that I have no recollection of Mum being taken to the hospital or even being told that she was unwell. I guess this was part of the weird dynamic of my parents' British heritage. Keeping up appearances is a very British problem. They were unable to ask for help and having to admit that things were not working was seen as a major failure. Keep calm (on the outside) and carry on. The problem with this is that you are solely dependent on your limited abilities. Dad was unable to help Mum, and we, as children, were unable to fill the void, so Mum's condition continued to worsen.

When mum was manic, she would do extreme and bizarre things like move all, and I mean all, the furniture out of the living room to outside. She reasoned that she believed that being more like Aboriginals and living outside was necessary. Look, I don't entirely disagree, but, well, you can see how manic her behaviour could become. One time, she became obsessed with wanting to kill my dad. She would take me outside and pick up a star picket and throw it like a javelin, telling me, "This is how I'm going to kill your father." Her delusions were violent, and she was completely detached from any form of reality during these moments.

I have fond memories of car trips with Dad to pick Mum up from Hobsons Park (psychiatric ward). I craved time with Dad, and spending an hour with him in a car was an absolute treat. We would go to Maccas on the way, which was also something to look forward to. A date with Dad and junk food - what a perfect plan!

We would collect Mum from the main entrance of the hospital. Dad would go into the reception, and I would wait in the car.

Mum would shuffle out escorted by a nurse. She was subdued and appeared mildly sedated. I expect she would have been fed a buffet of medication on her visits, as well as receiving Electric Shock Therapy (ECT). Mum's condition eventually became unmanageable for Dad, and given the era (80's), there was still truly little understanding about treatments and external support. There was an awful stigma around people with severe mental health conditions - they were threats to the community, unpredictable, and violent. To be fair, without understanding and proper consistent care, maybe this is the case for some, but for most people it's a life of torment and isolation, built on fear and delusion.

Later, in my twenties I asked Dad if Mum had stayed, would he have continued to stay married to her. Dad's response impacted me greatly. "I would have made it work until all of you had finished school." I believe that they genuinely loved each other. Even after the divorce, whenever I spoke to either of them, they would ask me about the other - just to make sure they were doing okay. I boil it down to two emotionally broken people who did not have the strength to weather the storm. Every marriage will be tested and challenged, and you need more than hope to make it work. You need to be brave and humble to ask for help; you need trust to let others in and fight with you for the marriage, and you need the skill, or at least the ability to learn new ways, to get through the fire. Everything was against this marriage, and it was destined to fail.

In 1989, Mum's parents offered to fly her back to England, but on a one-way ticket. Who knows what those conversations were like? Was that what Mum wanted? Was it Dad reaching out for help? Was it Dad admitting defeat? I honestly don't think a great deal about those questions. They are no longer relevant and there is no way of ever knowing.

Dad never sat any of us down to explain what was happening. He never explained her illness, the reason why she was always in the hospital, and he never indicated when we would see her again. As I'm writing this, I'm thinking he never had answers to any of these questions anyway. He was desperately trying to navigate a course that he had never planned to take.

This cycle of pain and suffering within my parents' relationship had an expiry date. The ship was on course to sink. Mum and Dad separated and divorced when I was seven. And Mum, at the request of her own parents, returned home to England.

My siblings and I with Mum, 2023

Mum never visited Australia again, the pain was simply too much for her. My siblings and I have taken many trips over to England to visit her over the years and have tried to maintain meaningful relationships with her. It took many years for Mum's mental health to stabilise. When she first returned to England, at times months would pass between hearing from her as she was still suffering from breakdowns, having to be hospitalised for treatment and care.

Chapter 3

Marmalade Toast

I vividly remember going with Dad to the airport to say goodbye to Mum.

"Mum's going back to England for a holiday," Dad told me. This was another one of Dad's *greatest parenting moments*. With this information, I was not fazed by Mum leaving; I was more excited about going to the airport! Dad said that we were going to have breakfast at the airport, so my focus was on the marmalade jam and toast I was going to have in the cafeteria. I knew the marmalade came in those little condiment packets, which in my seven-year-old brain was one of the greatest inventions ever! I still get excited about condiments that are individually packaged when I travel. They're like individually wrapped presents you get to unwrap. So, you can see why bidding my Mum farewell was low on my priority list at the time.

I remember Dad saying to me, "Say goodbye to your Mum now," as she was about to walk through to the departure lounge. Dad never saw Mum again, and it would be seven years before I was to see her again. Do you know - I didn't even hug her; I simply waved and said goodbye. I was used to her going away for extended periods at various times of my life, so in my mind this wasn't any different. This happened often and Mum usually came back after being away for a while, so I didn't see what the big deal was. Also, I never had a strong connection with Mum physically or emotionally, so it wasn't natural for me to want to hug her.

Although as a child you generally know the truth of what's going on most of the time, you also take what your parents say as gospel. For years, I expected Mum to return home. "Bloody long holiday," I would think to myself. But Dad never explained why she had left or that it was a permanent arrangement.

Chapter 4

New Home Life

For a while, it felt like it was just me and Dad. My siblings were still at home but living out their adolescent dreams, so most of the time our worlds were in different orbits.

I have fond memories of my second-oldest brother, Rod. He would take me motorbike riding, bush walking, and terrorise me at night by chasing me in the dark. I still have a very real fear of the dark because of this, but it's a fear attached to some incredibly fun memories, too.

Some of my early memories of my sister Anna were of her teaching me horse riding and going with her to pony club events. Dad was the BBQ man at the pony club, so I always spent the time hanging around him and wandering around watching my sister compete in various riding events.

Our family life became a sort of functional routine after Mum left. After school, I walked to Dad's workplace and played around in his office, waiting for him to finish his day. Dad worked a lot, and it's where, I believe, he felt most confident and comfortable. His work was predictable to a certain degree, and Dad was well-respected in his role as a consultant engineer. He worked hard at his job, and he worked hard at home.

Living on five acres in a small town called Longford meant there was always maintenance to be done and various projects on the go. I loved helping Dad in any way I could. Partly because I got to spend time with him, and partly because I genuinely enjoyed being outside helping, going to do the grocery shopping, feeding the animals, and "working" in the shed with Dad. Dad had set aside my own set of tools, which meant I could tinker away with him while he constructed actual architecture like garden beds and a chicken coop.

When I was tall enough, which was when I was around eight years of age, I began to mow the lawns for Dad, which I found extremely satisfying. At first, Dad would monitor my progress to make sure I was safe and doing the job according to his standards, ensuring I wasn't making my version of crop circles. Like any good parent, at some point, Dad was satisfied with my ability to mow the lawn as a responsible eight-year-old and trusted me to get the job done by myself. I must have qualified as the youngest mower girl in our area. Dad also showed me how to refuel the mower, which meant I didn't need him to help me at all. Weirdly, though, as an adult, it took Dad years to trust me with driving his car.

Dad did his absolute best to be there for us and provide for us. He had a strong belief that private education was essential for giving us the best opportunities in our future. We all attended Gippsland Grammar in Sale, which was close to where we lived. Being an Anglican school, religious education was a core subject, together with regular chapel services. We had a wonderful vicar named Caroline who made learning about God enjoyable. Caroline did a remarkable job of teaching the ethical principles of Christianity to young children. For me this was quite possibly the beginning of a time of wondering. The time we spent at the Chapel service was an opportunity to propel my thoughts further. I never remember anything that was said in a service, but I distinctly remember gazing at the stained-glass windows.

The pictures displayed in the stained glass were detailed images of Jesus and His disciples.

My imagination was captured by these images and in those moments, thoughts around what was playing out at home, worries about school, or about anything else, evaporated; focusing on these images created peace amid the storm.

Somehow, I had this idea in my head that you were meant to go to church outside of school. I came home from school one day and boldly asked Dad if we could go to church over the weekend. Other kids were asking for the latest toy or to go to a theme park - not this naive little poppet! It might have been the sense of peace I felt, or maybe a deep knowing that God and church were necessary and worth exploring further. I'm not sure, but to me it was simple - I had been told about God, therefore I should know God for myself.

There was something so attractive and fascinating about the idea of God. Dad ended up taking me to church just once on a weekend, the same church where we had our school chapel services. I was delighted that he had taken me. It was as special as it was a rare occasion to be doing something with Dad outside of home or school. I had such a feeling of peace and was captivated by the dazzling colours of the stained glass and the stories they told. I paid no attention to the message that was shared from the important robed person at the front; the message I was listening to was one told to me through the imagery I was focused on. The love of Jesus as He sat and taught His disciples; the care of Jesus as He carried a lone lost lamb; the reverence of His nature as Jesus gave Himself to His Father in Heaven. I understood later that these moments of deep contemplation were the starting point of a deep desire within me to know God personally.

Although home life wasn't perfect with three teenagers, one seven-year-old, and a single dad, it was home, and at times it was an absolute circus. My siblings were learning to drive and going to parties, and I was exploring the bush and swimming in water holes. Dad was reading Beatrix Potter stories to me at night, then picking teens up in the wee hours of the morning.

During this time of raising a family and re-establishing what our family looked like without Mum, Dad was going through the process of divorce and attaining legal custody as permanent carer for me. He gained full custody of me through the courts, but my siblings were old enough not to get caught up in this part of things. Reading the court documents much later in life, the proceeding seemed very straightforward. Mum, now living in England, would have no legal support, and who knows what her mother and father were advising her. I guess that her mother did not want her daughter to be seen as "the single mother in the village." The schizophrenic woman who lives in torment of not seeing her family is a much better look. Good choice, Grandma!

So, the new family unit was established. It was now Dad, my older siblings and I at home; but that would soon change as my brothers and sister left home to make their own way in life.

Chapter 5

And Then There Was One

In 1990, the gas company ESSO merged with Mobil, which saw the relocation of its head office from Sale, Gippsland, to Melbourne, a three-hour drive away from our home. This made a massive impact on the Gippsland area as families employed by the company and established in the Sale area had to relocate to the city. Economically, the area benefited greatly from the large income families. Consequently, many small businesses were forced to close, leaving the main street looking more like a ghost town than a small country town.

The impact of this merger on our family was massive. My brothers were then aged eighteen and nineteen and beginning to live independently. My sister, Anna, was in her final years of high school. I was only eight years old (nearly nine) when even more change came upon our family. Dad decided to move to Melbourne to follow his work, but instead of relocating the whole family, he decided to hire a nanny to care for me (and sometimes my sister) during the week while he was at work in Melbourne. He would return home on the weekends.

I was still very young, so Dad didn't want to disrupt my schooling and wanted us to continue to grow up in the country. So, with little discussion or conversation, Dad moved to Melbourne, and I was left in the care of a nanny. I don't remember him talking to me at all about his move to the city, I just knew he wasn't buying a house but rather staying in a one-bedroom motel room during the week. He may have spoken more to me about the changes that were taking place, but I was more focused on the scary fact that another parent was leaving rather than understanding why he was leaving.

The first nanny Dad hired was, in a word, awful. In the beginning, I was excited about someone new coming to live with us, but she had low tolerance for my sister and me. My sister was seventeen and very much her own person at this stage, not wanting or needing care from a stranger.

The following story will give you a glimpse into this nanny's character: my sister lived in the rumpus room or bungalow, which was outside the main house and attached to the garage. (Dad originally built it as an office space, but my older sibling soon invaded it, recognising that it was, in fact, a waste of office space and far more suited to a party crib. Poor Dad, a mild-mannered Englishman raising outgoing social sponges). My sister and the nanny did NOT get along. To my recollection, there were no fighting or disagreements; I just don't think my sister needed or wanted a stranger to interfere with our lives, so she continued taking care of herself.

One day, my sister had friends over, and they decided that they wanted cigarettes but couldn't drive or purchase cigarettes due to their age. The edgy, rebellious teens conceived a plan to get the nanny to drive to the shops for them. They consumed all the milk in the house, forcing a trip to the shops - clearly a well-laid plan by these wily teenagers. Well, the plan failed and ended badly. The nanny confronted my sister and her friends in the rumpus room. This confrontation ended with the nanny storming back into the house and locking all the doors, banishing my sister from entering her own home. The standoff had begun. Where was I? I was in the house watching everything unfold! When the doors were locked and war was declared, I was extremely confused and frightened, as this relative stranger had locked me in the house with her! With all due respect to the nanny, but we were probably responsible for her having a nervous breakdown later. The poor woman resigned by the end of the week.

Dad was beside himself, and he called my second eldest brother, Rod, to come home and bring some order into the place. Rod had moved out with his girlfriend and was attending university. The two had met in high school and were on their own "building a life together adventure." Rod had started to create his own life outside the chaos but was very much the dependable son during this time. Rod tried to reason with the nanny, but to my satisfaction, she was gone! Rod was the stable one in the family that Dad knew he could rely on. Even at eighteen, going to university, living his own life... when Dad needed another adult to help, he could always depend on Rod.

Dad even asked Rod to give me the puberty talk! What a horrendous idea that was! A teenage boy giving a pre-puberty girl the birds and the bees talk! Rod was smart enough to offload this task to his girlfriend. It was still mortifying for me. My childhood bubble dramatically and painfully popped all around me as Rod giggled and made smart remarks in the background while his girlfriend delivered the news that I would soon enter womanhood. I'd like to state here that due to the lack of female influence in my life, I promise you I had literally no clue as to what changes lay ahead of me. Our house was crazy, but my childhood bubble was my protective shield. I went from believing that you could get pregnant from kissing, to finding out what my body would suffer every month! But this was my big brother filling the gaps as best he could. To be fair, I'm very thankful that Rod stepped up the way he did. He was, and still is, a great representation of a solid man. He protected me and probably shielded me from things that were taking place within our home...as well as being a tormenting brother. Who knows how things would have turned out if he hadn't stepped up.

My sister finished school only a few months later and moved to Melbourne. She had no real plan except to have an adventure. She soon met her best friend and the love of her life! He was a city boy who also needed to make a way to new beginnings. The two left the Melbourne lifestyle after a year and moved interstate to New South Wales, working on farms picking fruit, running pubs, working in abattoirs; whatever was needed to start an adventurous life together. They got married at the age of twenty-one. Looking back, they only have fond memories and hilarious stories of building a humble life together. Their relationship is, to me, a wonderful example of a beautiful marriage.

My eldest brother was infrequently living at home at this stage. On a less desirable pathway, he was already getting into trouble with the police, taking large amounts of money from Dad, and generally making poor choices (to put it nicely). When he was good, he was caring and protective, but when he was off, he was violent and aggressive.

I remember one night, Dad was forced to call the police. Dad was outside, as I think the two had been fighting, and my eldest brother came running inside. I had been asleep but woke up to the sound of him punching the door of the linen cupboard (which was just outside my room). I don't ever remember feeling scared that night, just confused. I stepped out of my bedroom, and he just looked at me and kept punching the door. I can't remember exactly what he said, but he was gloating and encouraging me to look at the door he was destroying. When the police came, he ran down the hallway to the laundry, which led outside. I, for some reason, ran after him simply to follow. If memory serves me, Dad was still outside, but I'm not sure why he stayed there. Maybe there was more going on outside, maybe he was injured, I don't remember. There was no one else in the house, so I had no idea what I was meant to do. He was my brother. He had temporarily lost his mind, but I had no one else to give me direction. The door that led outside had a glass window in it. My brother ran up to the door and punched the glass as hard as he could. His hand penetrated the window, sending glass flying everywhere. I was behind him, stunned and confused.

He turned to me, showing off his arm, which was bleeding profusely. He laughed and said, "Look! Look!" waving his arm in front of me. He ran outside, where he was met by the police. I stayed inside. The last thing I remember was the bloody pattern on the ground, the lasting portrait of a night hallmarked by chaos and pain.

My eldest brother and his girlfriend moved out soon after, so there were no more memorable nights like that, although the behaviour continued, just not in our backyard or home.

So let me break this down for you. Dad relocated to Melbourne for work. My sister and second eldest brother had moved out, now living in Melbourne. And my eldest brother had also moved out of home but was still living in the area. Then there was one – just me, left in the nest, far too young to spread my wings but still desperately needing the protection of the family. The love deficit was great. I didn't understand why everyone had left.

What was wrong with me? Was there something wrong with me? Was I a bad child in a good world?

Dad managed to find a second nanny, so there were no other family members, just me and a new nanny.

Chapter 6

Shadows

When I was very young, I spent most of my time outside. We lived next to State bushland, so to me it was my own personal adventure playground. I spent hours wandering around playing out my imaginary explorations. Climbing trees, collecting bugs, and tadpoles. Dirt was the most common foundation for my skin. Whether I was lying in the grass watching eagles flying or uncovering a scorpion's nest, I was in my happy place when I was outside. When Dad and my siblings were still living at home, I had a sense of hope. Hope that regardless of all the fighting and painful events, we were still a family, and this family wanted me.

Dad moving to Melbourne was the beginning of a downward spiral for me. As an eight-year-old rationalising why everyone was moving away, I began to believe one thing: "no one stays by you forever," and "eventually people leave you." The seed of rejection was planted in fertile soil – and it grew. When people feel pain, they often look for a form of escapism. Rest assured, at eight years old, I wasn't about to stick a needle into my arm or turn to alcohol. My escape was TV and food. The freedom I found from being outside in nature's glory was quickly replaced by the dark shadows of the media and the comfort of food. Within twelve months, I went from an energetic average child to being overweight with zero confidence. To make matters worse, my brother Rod took me to get a haircut, which was the worst idea. Brothers should not oversee feminine needs. I came out with a magnificent bowl cut. A fat kid with a bowl cut does awful things for their self-esteem.

I would binge-watch TV. Bear in mind this was the late eighties, the era of free-to-air viewing. Basically, you watched the same show at the same time as everyone else. You would anticipate watching the next episode of whatever series you were into - The Cosby Show, Full House, Oprah, or Days of Our Lives. There could be a day or a week in between episodes. Watching multiple different shows during the afternoon was normal, and the couch potato slumped in front of the screen was in charge of what was watched. The TV was this generation's babysitter. Many parents assumed that what you were watching wasn't harmful, that it was a form of education, planting and developing ideas and beliefs in susceptible minds.

One of the shows I was hooked on was 'Degrassi Junior High.' This show was known as the 'pioneer of teen drama'. The show was developed in Canada by a non-union, independent production company. They developed the show in response to what they perceived to be 'a lack of proper educational programming targeted toward teenagers.'

Degrassi presented its package as relatable to the audience. Most of the characters showcased in the show were teens (who were not actors) creating something more believable for the audience. There was no set cast that played the same group of fifteen-year-olds for five years straight. The characters changed from season to season, and even episode to episode. The producer's aim was to confront relevant social issues that teens were confronted with - drugs, teen pregnancy and abortion, shoplifting, alcoholism, child abuse, homosexuality, and suicide. It was not light-hearted in the least. Maybe as an eight-year-old I was looking for something and someone to relate to, something that 'got me' and this show was what I latched onto.

Ideas have consequences, and ideas lead somewhere. With no one to talk to about the deep pain that was beginning to fester inside me or no one to look up to for any form of direction, I found people on TV who were not afraid to express their pain and have real talks about the issues they were facing.

There was one episode I clearly remember watching. One of the main characters was struggling with depression and withdrew from his friends. He battled with self-confidence and self-worth and at the end of the episode the young man committed suicide as a solution to his internal battle. His friends reacted with shock as none of them knew how dark his world was. This image of a much-loved character suddenly deleted from the show abruptly opened my eyes to mortality and the choice of life.

I was already questioning my own worth and purpose with feelings of rejection, fuelled by the belief of worthlessness simmering away in the back of my mind. Now the idea that our very existence might be a matter of choice slipped into the vortex of my mind, creating an even darker haze around my thoughts.

With no way of being accountable for my thoughts, this revelation of choice was stored in my mind and with it the accumulating evidence that justified worthlessness.

Moving forward to another life changing and inspiring episode of Degrassi Junor High - the topic of homosexuality and transgender was presented. This was the eighties, a sexualised era infiltrating every area of society. This episode was depicted by main characters describing their internal struggle with identity and developing a "knowing" that who they are was trapped within themselves. The feelings of not belonging or fitting into the status-quo and having to cover up their true self was part of the messaging in this episode.

This got my attention! I believed that I was not normal or average. I was taller and now fatter than all my female peers. I always preferred being outside rather than in a classroom. I always preferred the company of the boys at school, mainly due to the energetic play. I had older brothers, and, in my head, I was more like them. I was the only child at school with, not only a broken family, but a complex situation that anyone at the tender age of eight or nine would struggle to explain to another person.

My mother was absent, and her health made her representation of femininity undesirable. I felt a sense of responsibility towards Dad watching him fight, and at times fail, with our family's situation. Pain and fear ultimately separated me from others. I was like the characters on the show! I was trapped, I was an outcast, and my problems were too big to solve. I started to believe that changing who I was could set me free from this torment. What if I truly was a boy? Surely, I could fit into that mould, and it would feel more natural. This idea was filed right next to thoughts of rejection, worthlessness, and all-encumbering fear.

The thing with shadows is you don't notice them until complete darkness has covered the space you occupy. Shadows don't affect your ability to function as you are not focused on the shadows. You are focused on the day-to-day tasks, and on areas that still have light in them. If left unattended, your thoughts grow and become strong and evolve into beliefs, and like drawing all the curtains in a house, these thoughts block out the light, thereby blocking out the truth. Darkness enters and now you respond to the darkness and obey its demands due to the fear of uncertainty that it brings.

The shadows were real and becoming darker for me. At such an early age, I became focused on ideas that seemed like solutions to a true absence of belonging.

Chapter 7

New Options

Dad needed a new nanny to fill the position of carer within the home after the express exit of the previous one. This was way before LinkedIn and Job Seek; this was the modern dark ages of the 80's and 90's, before the internet. Dad placed an ad in the local paper, and there was an answer within days. Val was a local woman but had recently returned from working as a nanny in Canada where she had looked after a young girl for many years. A well-qualified, well-travelled, and very experienced woman. And let's be frank, being available to start straight away may have been the most outstanding part of her resume for Dad. Val Hall was hired as the new nanny.

My first impression was not great. I had only one experience with a strange woman responsible for looking after me, and it had left a taste of fear in my mouth. What if she was the same? What if she was worse? What if all nannies were assembled in a nanny factory? They weren't real humans; they were manufactured to manage children and suck the fun out of the air with their hash stares and disappointing tones.

Val looked to be the same age as the previous nanny. To a child anyone over the age of twenty was old, so this Val person was old! She drove a little white car, just like the prototype. Glasses - check. Grey hair - check. Experience with "caring" for children (unlikely story), and the weirdest similarity, which I promise I am not making up - both women were missing their right pinkie toe! Seriously, if that doesn't scream clone, I don't know what does. I was scared. My sister was now absent from my story as she had moved to Melbourne to expand her horizons. It was just me, now nine years old, and the new nanny-bot.

I think it only took me one week to quickly discover that Val was human, and concerns of a weird nanny version of the Terminator were put aside. Val was vibrant, energetic, and enthusiastic about life. She was and is one of the strongest women I know. While caring for me, she experienced devastating loss within her own family, together with other personal struggles. Yet she still consistently built a stable life around me.

Val was unapologetic about her faith in God; it was part of who she was. It wasn't necessarily through direct conversation that her faith was conveyed; it was more in the way she cared for others. We were constantly in her little white Daewoo car, belting down the highway with a casserole on the back seat, secured for delivery to someone in need of a home-cooked meal. As Val had grown up in the area and her family went back generations, she seemed to know, or know of, everyone. This was vastly different from the family I knew, which was not knitted into the wider community and my extended family was in England. My world had exploded into something far bigger than what I was used to, and it was life to me. Watching Val be so aware of others and doing the simplest things to show care and love was what captured my attention.

After school Val would pick me up and it was rare we'd go straight home. We would be on our way to someone's home to either deliver a meal which Val had cooked during the day, or to spend time with someone who needed a listening ear, or to babysit someone else's children. This effervescent woman had a heart for others and expressed this clearly through her actions.

The next bazaar thing that began happening was people would come over to our house! Previously our home was unpredictable with Mum suffering from schizophrenia. Visitors were a rarity and not a relaxing event. I remember Dad having a colleague and his wife over once. This was when I discovered that we had 'good' china. How English. Dad had a full set of intricately decorated china that was only used on special occasions. Dad spent time setting the table, as well as cooking a three-course dinner for his guests.

The thing I remember most was how tense Dad was. Everything had to be perfect - the setting, placemats, centre piece, different cutlery for different courses, and the crystal glassware. The timing of the event ran like you would expect an engineer to conduct an event, and the food was well planned. Perhaps because food is so exciting to me, I remember the details of Dad making prawn cocktails, delicately displayed in little glass bowls. I do believe that Dad wanted to connect with and enjoy the company, but he lacked the confidence to do so. As a result, he would deliberate over the details of hosting rather than find enjoyment in the company. In his later years Dad always said that he wasn't good with people and didn't know how to talk to them. In my opinion, he had much to offer, but his thoughts about himself and how others viewed him tainted his ability to build meaningful relationships.

Now, a new culture was beginning to be built in our home where people would come to our house and bring something to contribute to dinner. We would talk and share in the moments together without a time limit or schedule. Val would often have people from the church she attended come over for dinner.

They would bring their children too, which I got so excited about, as these kids who were not in a private school uniform and did not question where my family was. The pressure was off me, and I was able to be my authentic, dorky self. These new faces soon became friends, and I was excited knowing that my home was being filled with precious people that I was slowly beginning to love.

The children who came over were all around my age, so it was natural that we soon became friends, and this added to the joy of these moments for me. I had friends at school, but no one whom I felt excited about. I was more of a shadow with my friends at school, trying to be accepted while covering up everything I was ashamed of. However, I was not a quiet kind of gal. I vividly remember my grade four teacher, Mrs. Mac, calling me an eggbeater because I could be quick witted and a bit of a stirrer at times. Yet, at the same time, I did my best just to fit in and not be outstanding in any way.

I was a chatterbox in class. One time, I pushed the limit with my teacher. She had already moved me to sit next to someone else, which I took to mean I had a fresh audience to entertain. The next minute, I was in detention for talking! Detention at school was to stand outside the staff room for half of lunchtime. We had to stand upright against the stone-cold brick wall; it was stone-cold like my teacher's soul!

I had often seen other children enduring the elements while serving their time. The 'incarcerated' were almost always boys. Now I was one of the convicted, being punished for finding more exciting things to learn about, rather than listening to the drone of an uninspiring warden. At first, the public shame was overwhelming. Four other boys who had regular appointments with the wall were already at their posts. They knew the drill.

But for me, thoughts were rushing through my head like "What if my friends see me?" "What if I can't find my friends after I am released?"

On this day, Nick White, who was well-used to the drill of lunchtime detention, whipped out a tennis ball he had swiped from PE class - probably part of the reason he was serving time. We proceeded to play a sensational game of down-ball, timing our shots so as not to be caught by teachers coming in and out of the staff room. It was just me and the boys, and it turned out to be a super fun lunchtime!

I learned a lot that day. I had no desire to be segregated; being included and to fit in was all I wanted from my peers. I learned to scale it back in class, and to not ask questions. Asking questions showed others that you were inferior. You keep your thoughts and ideas to yourself as you might be wrong and be judged for your contribution.

I already felt odd and was beginning to feel like an outcast. As a result, I didn't make close friends at school like other kids normally did. These new children entering my world and coming into my home were completely different from me. Maybe because it wasn't in a school setting, or maybe because we were building friendships without any other pressures being added to the equation, or maybe these were, quite simply, special friendships being formed.

As these were Val's church friends, the conversation orbited mostly around God and how each person was growing in God. No one was excluded from the conversations; even the children who came would share with their limited understanding of God and their faith in Him.

The school I was attending was Anglican-based, so I was aware of God and knew Jesus was real, but I had never heard about growing in God and knowing Him personally. And now, here I was watching a motley crew - young and old, from different walks of life, expressing their love for God with passion that left me in awe.

Val looked after me for four years, and in this time, I experienced what I think was a normal childhood. Normal in the sense of feeling safe, having sleepovers with friends, and going on day trips with other people's families. I didn't have to think about what we were doing as Val was dependable and consistent. Dad would come home every second weekend. I don't remember my siblings coming home much, so, for the first time, life was predictable and I was surrounded by kind and caring people.

Val and I, 2022

About a year after Val came to work for us as a nanny, we were in her Daewoo bolting down the highway to visit one of her friends. Val was in full swing conversation, most of which I don't remember, until the topic of God came up.

Val asked me one of the most profound questions that had ever been asked of me. "Do you want a relationship with God?" What the heck?! My thoughts were now abuzz. "God out there, the Creator of the universe? Can I have a proper relationship with Him?" I thought believing in God was just that, believing. I believed that He's out there and we all just had to try our best to be worthy of Him.

That split second caused a major glitch in my understanding - there was suddenly the possibility of a different choice. A different outcome was now presented to me. In that moment, I became very aware of the thoughts that were banging around in the back of my mind. They had been dormant as things around me were good and I had no time or need to focus on the shadows; but they were alive and well. So, when that question was put before me, "Would you like to have a relationship with God?" It was easy to say yes. Why? Because the alternative trajectory for my life was grim, and I knew it. The conversation in my head went like this: "You've got nothing to lose. You've already made your choice to end your own life at some point, so if God fails you, you're back to plan A. Jo, you've got nothing to lose."

I felt incredibly conscious about what was happening. Val was just the messenger. God Himself was inviting me into a relationship with Him. Val and I prayed, and I asked God to find His home in my heart. I asked God to forgive me, which I didn't fully understand. I just knew that not only was God real, but He knew who I was and wanted to make Himself known to me in a much deeper way than I could ever have imagined.

Chapter 8

Woman At The Well

There is a story in the Bible that tells of a woman who was an outcast and was shunned by her community. Women in that time would go in the morning to draw water from the wells before the heat of the day set in. This woman was drawing water during the middle of the day, indicating that she was not welcome to be with the other women. And to make matters worse, she met Jesus, who was of a different race and the two were not supposed to associate.

John 4:9 (NIV), *The Samaritan woman said to him, "You are a Jew and I am a Samaritan woman. How can you ask me for a drink?" (For Jews do not associate with Samaritans.)*

Jesus speaks to her, revealing His knowledge about her life and why she was an outcast. He also reveals the longing in her heart, the thirst that is never quenched.

John 4:13, *Jesus answered, "Everyone who drinks this water will be thirsty again, but whoever drinks the water I give them will never thirst. Indeed, the water I give them will become in them a spring of water welling up to eternal life."*
  The woman said to him, "Sir, give me this water so that I won't get thirsty and have to keep coming here to draw water."
  He told her, "Go, call your husband and come back."

"I have no husband," she replied.

Jesus said to her, "You are right when you say you have no husband. The fact is, you have had five husbands, and the man you now have is not your husband. What you have just said is quite true."

This woman was not an inconvenience to Jesus; she was hand-picked by God for this moment.

Jesus begins to reveal the truth to her. He begins to show her that she is acceptable before God, and that faith in the spoken word of God is what liberates a life and brings unity where unity is impossible.

John 4:23-26,28 (NKJV), But the hour is coming, and now is, when the true worshippers will worship the Father in spirit and truth; for the Father is seeking such to worship Him. God is Spirit, and those who worship Him must worship in spirit and truth."

The woman said to Him, "I know that the Messiah is coming" (who is called Christ). "When He comes, He will tell us all things."

Jesus said to her, "I who speak to you am He."

The woman then left her waterpot, went her way into the city, and said to the men, "Come, see a Man who told me all things that I ever did. Could this be the Christ?"

The woman left Jesus and immediately went and spoke about her encounter. Her heart was open, and she told people about what Jesus had told her about her life. Her response opened an entire region for Jesus and his disciples to not only pass through but were now welcomed to stay. Previously, Jews were not welcome in the region.

There is so much in this Scripture, but what I want to draw from this passage is that God revealed Himself to this woman. She was an outcast. She was ordinary. She was ashamed of her life, yet God saw her and revealed Himself to her. She went from seeing just a Jewish man to recognising the Messiah! Christ knew her in a way no one else did.

In the car that day with Val, He had revealed Himself to me! El Roi (the God who sees) had seen me and made Himself known to me. Not only that, but He knew me and saw me. Regardless of all the mess, shame, and fear, God still showed Himself to an eleven-year-old little girl living in an insignificant area, who showed no real potential, and who could not see any real future ahead. Yet God exposed His love for her in a way no one else could.

My response after saying yes to God was something I considered natural and normal - everyone needed to know about this God whose love is greater than you can fathom. When I went to school the following week, I was unashamed to tell my friends about God and how they could have a personal relationship with Him. I used those exact words, too. I can't imagine what fellow eleven-year-olds would have thought. "No thanks, I'm good with my family. My Mum and Dad are pretty good." "Nothing I need to be saved from over here."

I even wrote down a prayer so I could remember it and took it to school in case someone wanted to pray to God and ask Him to be a part of their life. I led a few school friends through this prayer, and I hope they genuinely wanted to know God like I did. However, there's a strong possibility that they obliged my invitation of prayer simply because they were bewildered by my forwardness - talking about God outside of the context of religious education and the formalities of school. Possibly no other student had needed to contemplate who God was to them personally. I wouldn't call what I was doing bold, confident, or courageous. It was more of a response to a newfound focus and an undeniable awakening to the truth of who God is.

I started going to church with Val on the weekends when Dad was away. Considering that this was a yearning of mine from much earlier in my life, I was keen to get into this whole "knowing God" more than ever. It was another mind-blowing experience to begin with. The motley crew of people that would occasionally meet at my house also gathered on Sundays, happily and of their own free will. Some families appeared quite conservative, others seemed very free-range.

There were disabled people and rough-looking sorts, and there were average-looking people who seemed to have their lives together. This was not an Anglican service. There were no stained-glass windows. The organ was ditched for a keyboard, and physical movement was encouraged. Finally, I couldn't get into trouble for fidgeting! Hymn number 27 was replaced with "I'm Trading My Sorrows". And the controlled delivery of a boring sermon was instead a message of truth and conviction.

I told my dad that I was going to church (though not in any detail). I considered myself to be a very honest person and open with my friends, but with family it was a different story. I was worried about what Dad would think. You see, with strangers and friends, you've got nothing to lose. If they don't like what you have to say, then you can easily distance yourself from them, and there's no love lost. However, with family, it's different. Especially when all you innately desire is a relationship and closeness with them. When you fear losing what fragments are left, you become very careful not to offend or disrupt for fear of being rejected and losing what you believe is most valuable to you.

I'm not sure what Dad thought about the whole matter, as anything outside of a 1950's version of church would have caused him some conniptions. I imagine that Dad was just thankful that, for the first time, no dramas were happening on the home front.

The only other family member I told was my eldest brother. He was living an independent life, but still occasionally came to stay. His response was amusing to me. He encouraged me to stop going to church and warned me off making friends in the church. Considering that he was on a very destructive pathway and consistently made poor choices, I found his words to be more of a confirmation, fuelling my desire to follow God more. What he was saying was, "Don't go down that pathway towards God. Follow me, my way is far more promising." But in my head, it was like, "Yeah, how about no? Thanks for the guiding words, big brother, but what you offer is not that attractive."

I was learning about God and how to have a relationship with Him. I was learning how to pray, how to worship, and how to study the Bible so it would reveal more of God. I was not just learning how to use these new tools, but to master them for the future. Like a Girl Guide (which I did endure for one entire year), you learn skills so that one day, when the weather changes, you are prepared and equipped to endure the storm.

Chapter 9

Weather Changes

The saying goes that all good things must come to an end, which is a very English thing to say. To my way of thinking, what it really meant was, 'Don't get too excited about life because we are all doomed anyway.'

What I mean to say is that life for me in those four short years Val looked after me was good, but change was always in the air. I was never going to live with Val forever, and eventually, Dad's situation was destined to change once more.

The first thing that indicated change was coming and that things were not as they seemed, was when I was taken to see a counsellor. You see, Val knew much more than I did about our family history. It was Val who eventually sat me down for the first time to explain why Mum had left. As I mentioned earlier, Dad simply told me that Mum was going on a holiday back to England. I knew that it wasn't true, but I wanted to trust Dad and believe that eventually Mum would come home. Val sat me down right at the beginning of her employment and told me the harsh truth in the most delicate way. My mother suffered from schizophrenia and went home to England to receive better care. Val also encouraged me to talk to my second-oldest brother, who was now at university studying psychology. She told me that he would have a better understanding of the condition. I never asked my brother any questions. More understanding of an illness doesn't change the fact that your mother left and wasn't coming back.

Val always encouraged me to write letters to my Mum but didn't make a big deal about it. I had questions, but nothing pressing, and there was nothing that constantly tormented me. I accepted that Mum was unwell and that England was the best place for her.

When I was twelve, and Val had been my nanny for three years, she spoke to Dad about booking me in to see a counsellor. This was a shock to me. A world crusher. I didn't realise I was broken; I didn't understand what a counsellor did except that they talked to people about their problems. In my mind, I was doing well. I was struggling academically at school, but a counsellor couldn't help with maths and English. I had friends, I was active, and I was feeling hopeful. Maybe it was because Val knew that change was coming, or maybe it was because I was about to go into high school. Perhaps I didn't realise that the way I was acting was very different from how I believed I was acting. I have no idea.

To my recollection, I only went a few times to see this counsellor. She was pleasant and seemed caring. Her room was lovely, with natural sunlight filling the room. There were coloured pictures on the wall and comfortable chairs to sit on. I only remember one session with her clearly. She asked me to draw a picture of what I was feeling on a normal day. I drew a picture of me walking through a beautiful landscape, the sun was shining. The sun was happy; I know this because I drew a smiley face on it with cool sunglasses. We've all done that drawing in the 90's, but when I drew myself, I was holding an umbrella with a rain cloud over my head. As I looked at that picture, the counsellor asked a few questions to clarify and helped me to understand what I had drawn.

"Is this you in the picture?" she asked.

"Yes, that's me."

"Do you feel like the sun shines everywhere except where you are?"

"That's how I feel."

In that moment, I understood that what was always around me was sadness. Those few years with Val and finding God were fun and exciting. The dark thoughts that had invaded my thinking were kept at bay, but they weren't gone; in fact, they were part of who I was. Deep down inside, they were what I believed about myself. These thoughts were just waiting for the perfect moment, and the right conditions to ambush me. I'm not sure why I never went back to see her; it wasn't an unpleasant experience, but it was confronting to acknowledge that I was a very sad pre-teen girl.

My first year of high school was, like many teens, tricky to navigate. You are herded from the smaller, more personal environment of primary school to the bigger pool of people and more responsibility. This is mixed with the expectation that your academic foundation is set from primary school. Now in high school, you are set to excel. Ummm … how about no?

Handy cap number one

Due to the chaos at home, I never had anyone to read with or to do extra work with me when I was falling behind. There was no time to help the youngest child in the family while the family was falling apart. At school, I struggled to understand the recipes for learning and fell further and further behind. In grade six, I was at a grade four level of reading and writing.

Handy cap number two.

I was behind the eight ball on the social rules that high school was established on. In primary school, you were friends with anyone who enjoyed the same games, who was funny, and who had good food to swap at lunchtime. I assumed that this code of conduct continued into high school. It was like a weird form of evolution that had taken place with all the other students over the holidays. Their focus was no longer on the innocence of getting along for the purpose of having fun; their focus was now on survival and domination! Nobody told me! It was like they had all gotten together over the holidays and discussed the social structure of year seven and forgot to inform me.

In primary school, I was a tomboy of sorts, taller than the other girls and about the same height as the boys. My interests were in physical play rather than the gossip and social planning that girls were inclined to do. In primary school, the boys were easier to understand socially, until testosterone suddenly kicked in and boys became like a man-child. No longer were they my equals. They were stronger and faster. I was displaced. I had no idea what was happening.

As the plague of puberty consumed every teenager I knew, I didn't understand why girls' emotions were so much more extreme in comparison to the boys. Or why the girls, who were becoming young women, wanted to talk about their emotions. I still wanted to create tactile things and to be active, not spending my days talking about hypothetical relationships. Why was I becoming more and more aware of my displacement and more and more self-conscious? I had no understanding of how hormone changes affected a young woman and how hormones could amplify our emotions. And what if those emotions were attached to a wrong thought? Then what? How do I navigate through that? Like so many kids my age I felt distressed and confused - you think you can run away and avoid the 'danger' of not fitting in, or that you can fight your way back into a place of safety by forcing your way into a social group, often at the cost of others. The reality for me was that I began to draw inwards and disconnect. Teachers saw this as a kid with a low attention span and ill-thought-out behaviour. 'Joanne, are you listening?' 'Joanne, think about what you are doing', were comments I often heard, if I was even listening. A mental disconnect, intertwined with a loss of hope and fear became a way of surviving.

Handy cap number three.

From day one, the social groups were very clear:

Popular kids - these are the ones who are usually nice, and everyone adores them, including the teachers.

The Jocks - mostly boys and a few insecure girls - these kids were mean and used intimidation to stay on top of the pecking order.

The nerds, or the academic kids - confident and slightly disinterested in the other social groups. They are secure in the knowledge that after school they would go to university and major in a science degree; this would be their time to shine. They know high school is just a mandatory part on the way to an environment that they will later come alive in.

And then there were the misfits - they weren't strong on anything except staying out of sight. This was where I sat - a misfit.

The only issue was that in a private school in the 90's, we were the minority - meaning I was the only misfit kid!

There was so much to adjust to in high school. The new social order meant new strategies to survive. I knew that if I stood up for myself or someone else, I would have a target on my back, mostly from the insecure jocks. Remember, their survival depended on ensuring there were no uprisings from other districts. Passive agreement became my method for managing high school.

During this time of transitioning into high school, Dad met someone and was in a new relationship. I was very happy for him as I desperately wanted him to feel loved and to stop being lonely. Dad started bringing his new partner, Louise, with him when he returned home every second weekend. His attention was quite obviously on Louise, so I began to feel replaced and lost within the relationship. Louise was from the city, which is where they had met, and they began to make plans to get married and move in together. By the end of the year, Dad was having a conversation with me about moving to the city.

"How would you feel about moving to live with Louise and me in the city?"

"Um, no thanks. I'm good here in Longford."

Note to all parents out there: If you have already made a plan that you need your children to comply with, don't ask them if they're on board with it; you're giving them a false impression that they have a choice in the matter. I was devastated when Dad turned around and informed me that I was moving, changing schools, and becoming part of a new family. Leaving my church and friends was the most crushing part of the move. I knew full well that you couldn't find those kind of friends just anywhere. They are special and unique. You can't replicate or replace people. I was not just moving away from familiar surroundings but away from people who had become a bedrock in my young life. I had found God and was beginning to understand for myself who He was. Now I would have to fend for myself and build new relationships in the city, of all places. I had to learn to survive in a new climate.

Chapter 10

Change And Adventure

I was genuinely happy for Dad. He had seemed lonely and was a good man who wanted and needed companionship. We moved to Mornington, which wasn't quite the city, but for me it was close enough. It was a nice reputable area on the peninsula that attracted 'toffee-nosed' people who wanted to buy houses with a coastal view. That view was indeed spectacular and became my saving grace.

We were not a toffee-nosed family. We were a mismatched, blended family, just trying to make a fresh start. Louise and her two children, James (25) and Fiona (18), were originally from England. The family had immigrated to Australia only a few years earlier. Louise had lost her late husband to suicide, and she had grown up in a very strict English home. Louise's parents and two brothers had already immigrated to Australia, so when the tragedy of her husband's death occurred, making a fresh start in Australia was the choice that made the most sense.

This new step-family was a completely different culture from the Verrill household. There was a lot of talk between siblings and their mother. They also gave each other a lot of physical affection. There were open conversations between all three members of the family. I never felt like we were a fully-fledged, united family. I guess that was understandable given our ages and that Dad and I moved into their house.

I was thirteen, turning fourteen, starting at a new private school in a new area. The school I attended was a little different as far as traditional private schools go. We had no uniform, just a dress code, and we were required to wear earthy colours such as greens and browns, basically. This school was like a boot camp for anyone preparing to live in Brunswick, followed by Byron Bay in their later years. It was situated in bush surroundings; there were plenty of native trees, with the classrooms nestled into pockets in the school grounds. The school had a strong Arts curriculum and tons of elective classes available. While I was there, I participated in team building challenges, textile art, poetry, outdoor ed activities, mechanics, and golf. Yes, golf. How private is that! I told you I was living where beautiful people lived. I did quite well with golf, too; maybe there was some class in my bloodline after all. All these classes were a great way to disconnect from the other pressures of academic performance. Apart from that, let's just say that of all the things those experiential classes covered, doing my tax return wasn't one of them. High school was hard; although I did find a good group of friends, and we stuck together, which was our survival plan for those formative years. Survival can only happen within a pack. If you stray from the herd, you become a target for the established social clusters. (Much like Lord of the Flies without the plane crash and the desert island.)

None of the teachers knew me or my family. I was no longer identified as the little sister of one of my siblings. Or Joe Verrill's (my father) youngest child. Even though I was a misfit at Grammar, I lived in the shadows of my siblings, who were social elites. This often worked in my favour, particularly with teachers.

So, here I was, a nomad in a private school that didn't have a uniform; so, we dressed to express!

Uniforms are great. There is no self-expression when you wear a uniform, except for those girls who wear their dresses nice and short, making focus hard for most boys. No, uniform meant full exposure to the fact that I had been raised by my dad, and that he had obviously given me no feedback on my dress sense. That would have been very helpful, Dad. Small blessing - there was no social media back then! Therefore, my fashion statements will never come back to haunt me. My usual get-up was one of Dad's old retro shirts, which I thought were cool. I still do, but the way I used to style them didn't do the shirts justice. Plaid pants with a slight flare... I did love those pants. Navy blue Doc Martins: I didn't want to wear the same as everyone else, that's why I never bought the traditional black Doc Martins. Funny thing was, even with black Docs, there was no chance of looking even remotely like what was in style or what other kids were wearing. I was inspired by mainstream bands like 'The Cranberries', 'Alanis Morrisette' Christian bands like 'Delirious' and 'Newsboys'. All a little bit edgy, all pushing a cause. Unfortunately, my interpretation of this edginess into fashion was predominantly a giant misfire.

I was still rocking the bowl cut by the way; I just couldn't come out of a hairdresser with any other style. Shame on those hairdressers! Why didn't anyone feel sorry for the oddly dressed child who was losing the battle with all the puberty changes? Surely, if you had a kid like me sit in your chair asking for "just a trim, please" (because I didn't know what else to ask for), you could have helped. If someone had asked me, "Would you like to try something new?" "Heck, yes!" would have been the answer. Anything other than this chubby version of 'He-Man!'

School was bearable and I managed to get by, passing with average grades. As each year rolled over, I began to drop more challenging subjects like maths and science.

I was still struggling, and some teachers noticed this. I had discussions with a teacher once, who informed me that they suspected I was dyslexic. Looking back, this made a lot of sense as learning to read never made sense to me, so I memorised words rather than learning phonetics and the 'rules' of spelling. However, I was never tested, and it was never explained to me what the word 'dyslexic' meant. I felt a new level of incompetence, and my confidence plummeted. There were no strategies to help me after that conversation; rather, it just confirmed in my thoughts that, yet again, I was different.

It wasn't until year ten that I was taught a very valuable lesson by two teachers. The first was Mr. Mashford, my business studies teacher. The correct title of the class was 'Small Business Enterprise Studies', SBES for short. He was a teacher who clearly preferred certain students, and it wasn't uncommon for him to make demoralising comments to those he didn't like. We had all been working on our end-of-semester assignments, and it was time for us to get our results for all our hard work. Mr. Mashford was sitting at his desk with a handful of papers, and he called each one of us to come and collect our work and receive a little feedback. When my name was called, I walked up, not thinking much except "I hope I get just a C for my grading." Mr. Mashford chuckled to himself as he handed back my assignment and said,

"I must have had one too many glasses of red wine when I was marking your work." He gave me a B+. I was pleased because this was much better than what I had expected, but Mr. Mashford's comment deflated my celebrations. It was like his expectations of me were so low that for me to receive a good assessment could only be as a result of his intoxication. So, in my head, my SBES teacher was not only a jerk but a self-proclaimed alcoholic!

Mrs. White was a brilliant English teacher in my eyes. She had given us a writing task and had given us two weeks to complete it. I handed mine in on time, which was surprising for me; I really must have liked Mrs. White. During our next lesson, she handed back all our writing pieces except for mine. When the class was over, she walked to the door with all the students as they moved to leave the classroom. Mrs. White pulled me aside as she stood with my writing piece in her hand. It had no grade written on it. My word, had I completely failed? Had I failed that badly it wasn't even worth the red ink in her pen to write an F? Mrs. White looked at me with kind, concerned eyes and said, "I know you can do better than this. You have one week to rewrite this piece." The response within me was utter joy! Mrs. White could see potential in me! She didn't know anything about me, but she could see something, something worth pushing for. I was being pushed for the first time to raise the standard and go further than what I was comfortable with. I felt a great sense of motivation from her encouragement and belief in me.

Those two teachers, Mr. Mashford and Mrs. White, both gave me a gift. The gift of choice. Whose words would I believe? Whose words would I follow? The choice to believe that I was stupid and my success in life was only accidental, or that I am capable. It would be uncomfortable and challenging, but I could go a lot further if I chose to.

Now, in year 10, I was still socially confused. I wanted to belong but didn't want to do all the things that came with high school acceptance. The parties, the drugs, the sex. Being a private school, drugs were plentiful and available. It wasn't the case of 'knowing the right people.' The 'right' people were in my class, and everyone knew who they were. They obviously listened hard to Mr. Mashford's business lesson, as they had a thriving enterprise.

Teens with raging hormones, with brains that are not fully developed, and social status to be claimed - this is the common world of parties in high school. I'd heard about what went on over the weekend at different people's houses, and my education rose to a whole new level. I was honestly terrified of stepping into that scene. There was no way I was going to get stuck at someone's house and be pressured into doing things I couldn't be sure I would say no to. None of it appealed to me. Thankfully, my friends at school didn't care that I didn't go to the parties, and our close friendship still enjoyed sleepovers with just the girls most of the time.

During my second year at this new school, in year 9, I began to volunteer for different things. I joined Amnesty International and spent many lunchtimes either writing letters to different governments in aid of freeing prisoners of war, or I was selling their merchandise in the city. Our teacher would drive us in, and we were allowed to wander around and sell the merchandise. I enjoyed doing this, meeting new people, chatting with them about Amnesty, and I was good at selling stuff.

I also volunteered at the Youth Resources Centre, where I gave my time to the Kids Help Line. This was a little more confronting, as part of the role was to hand out clean syringes. The thought of someone my age using needles broke my heart.

I found all these endeavours fulfilling, and they came naturally to me. I felt satisfied that I was helping someone somewhere, but I also felt a greater pull within me to do more.

For a fleeting moment, I wanted to join Greenpeace and save the whales! Then I read a story of a man who was a truck driver. While he was on the road, he talked to other truck drivers over the radio. They would share their struggles with depression and suicidal thoughts with him. He shared stories of talking people down from committing suicide. Suddenly, I wanted to be a truck driver! I wanted to help. I wanted to advocate. I was moved by people who were brave enough to walk with others through their dark times.

While living in Melbourne, I maintained my friendships back home in Sale, Gippsland. These friendships were relatively drama-free. I would be on the phone most nights talking to my best friends who were from my church. We would write letters to each other, which I still have to this day. (Teenage letters are priceless!) My friends back home were not experimenting with drugs and sex. They were in church, having crushes on church boys, and most importantly, still learning about God, Jesus, and the Holy Spirit.

Chapter 11

The Back End Of Nowhere

During my second year at Woodleigh (the posh school for would-be hippies who can afford shoes but choose not to wear them), my church back in Sale was planning a trip to Burke. Where is Burke? The back end of nowhere in the middle of New South Wales. What was there? A First Nations Church whose leaders had connected with my Pastors and had built a lasting friendship with them. The plan was wild. The plan was to shut the church in Sale for two weeks while we drove to the outback in convoy for three days. While we were there, we worked with the elders of the church in Burke and ran church meetings in the middle of the housing estate.

As a fifteen-year-old, I had very little concept of how crazy this trip was going to be. In my head I was going on a two-week road trip to have adventures in the outback with my best friends. The trip was planned for the school holidays, so Dad was fine with letting me go. Dad had no idea what type of town Burke was. It is, in fact, one of the wildest towns in New South Wales and is well known for crime and poverty. I did not know that at the time. It wasn't until I was well into my thirties that it dawned on me how crazy this trip really was.

It turned out to be life-changing in all the right ways. The purpose of what church truly was became so clear to me during this trip. Life with God is meant to be an adventure and meant to be lived with a tribe of people! The time that we spent with the Aboriginals pastors and the people from their church impacted me in a most profound way. In my narrow-minded, English way of thinking, your biological family was who you were loyal to, and everyone else came second. But here I was in an Aboriginals community, slowly getting absorbed into their 'family'; we all were.

By the end of the trip, all of us 'young ones' were calling any elder 'aunty' or 'uncle,' and I was being referred to as 'sis.' It's important to note that this is a community that doesn't welcome strangers. If you are welcomed in, you are family, and that's how it felt. Through God, through His Spirit, we were all standing together. It wasn't culture or colour; it was our united love for God.

There are so many hilarious and moving stories from this trip that I simply couldn't do them justice by writing about them in this book, and many of the stories probably break an excessive amount of OH&S rules. I will, however, share this one story, which showed me the Father heart of God.

One night, we were having a church meeting in an open-air tent. We worshipped together all night singing, 'He is Lord.' There were over one hundred people who gathered from the housing estate. Pastor Henry (who was from Burke) was sharing a message and invited people to come to the front for prayer. It was hot and dusty, and you could smell a distinct earthy smell in the air. Pastor Henry, a small-framed Aboriginals man, came over to me as I responded to the call to come for prayer. He put his hand on my shoulder and began to share with me what God was showing him.

"I see you and your family at the altar. Your whole family is there with their arms raised, worshipping God."

He spoke softly yet firmly as if he knew my family was not yet walking with God. This moved me to tears as this was 'Big God' speaking directly to me. El Roi (the God who sees) was speaking directly to me about the people I loved, but who I also felt detached from. God loved them even more than I did, and He had a distinct plan for them.

At fifteen, I experienced church 'unusual'. We had come together with only one purpose - to lift up the name of Jesus in the forgotten back blocks of New South Wales. After this trip, God had my full attention. My mind was racing with the possibilities of what God could do. My heart was full because of strengthened relationships. Coming home after this trip and returning to school wasn't that big of a deal for me anymore, as I knew without a doubt that it was only a matter of time before I would return to my hometown of Sale.

Chapter 12

Trust That The Storm Will Pass

I loved God dearly, and although I didn't really know what it meant to give my life to God, I knew I didn't want to give up what I had experienced in church already. The other part, I believe, that contributed to my ability to resist the rituals of high school, was a genuine fear of being taken advantage of. Why deliberately put yourself in a situation where a boy can use you and be entertained by you? No, thank you. I recognise that this is not a regular train of thought for a teenage girl. But all credit goes to my circus of a childhood. In some ways I grew up very quickly and became streetwise as a result. Staying away from people who could expose my shame and potentially reject and hurt me was my superpower!

High school was a wild ride of learning who to trust and who not to trust. Learning how to avoid bullies and learning that at camp, everyone was friends, but back in the school yard, segregated groups quickly reassembled.

I was a tomboy of sorts, still battling my bowl haircut and dressing in comfortable clothes - as I mentioned before, sometimes hand-me-downs from Dad's wardrobe paired with Doc Martin's and not particularly feminine. Different kids began to ask me if I was gay; this was challenging, and I certainly wrestled with it. Were people seeing something I didn't? Could they read my mind as I struggled to understand my sexuality? Between thoughts that I had about myself, and questioning whether I was born in the wrong body, made me wonder if they were right.

Instead of accepting that I was the cover girl for awkward teen girls, people felt the need to categorise me to understand and accept me. As an adult, I recognise this as a natural human instinct. If you can label something, you can understand it better and therefore accept or reject it. It is only through God's word that we understand how to truly care for others.

John 15:12-14 'This *is My commandment, that you love one another as I have loved you. Greater love has no one than this, than to lay down one's life for his friends. You are My friends if you do whatever I command you.* '

And through the understanding of the Word, through the Holy Spirit, we can come to accept people as they are.

Mathew 11:28 '*Come to Me, all you who labour and are heavy laden, and I will give you rest.*'

All God asks of us is to come. Come into His presence because in His presence is where healing and restoration begin. I had not known this as a teenager, so my peer's words affected me and confirmed my festering thoughts of confusion.

While I endured the school years, home life was once again getting wobbly. In 1995, Dad had heart surgery. His heart had potentially been damaged by strokes which had not been properly investigated. Dad was soon scheduled for a triple bypass. While in surgery, they made that a quadruple bypass. Typical Englishman, always wanting to get the best deal - four for three deal.

Dad's recovery didn't go well. It was the first time I believe Dad felt genuine fear for his life. I remember going to visit him in the hospital while he was in the ICU hooked up to tubes and monitors. When he saw me, he began to cry. Seeing your dad, the rock of your world, cry is heartbreaking and ever so scary.

Dad couldn't speak due to the damage the breathing tube had caused when it was removed. Instead, he took my hand and with his finger, he wrote "I love you" in the centre of my palm. I knew Dad was fearful of not coming out of the hospital and just wanted his children near him. At the end of the day, that's what every father wants - his children close to him. A father doesn't care what condition his children are in when they come close to him, he wants to show his love and care for them. And I believe in his own way, that's what Dad was doing in that moment. He returned home after some weeks, but his health never returned to normal after that surgery. He returned to the hospital twice after that with an infection. He was forced to retire from the gas industry, and I believe this crushed Dad beyond repair. He had lost a big part of his identity and purpose, which was embedded in his career.

My stepmother, Louise, was finishing a bachelor's degree while looking for more work during this time. The relationship between Dad and my stepbrother, James, was tense, and they were becoming less tolerant of each other, and my step mum was continually trying to support both parties. The time bomb was ticking.

Suddenly, my step mum made a snap decision, or maybe she just snapped. She decided to look for work in Western Australia (a two-to-three-day continuous drive from one side of the country to the other). I still, to this day, don't really understand the logic of this move, but I do know that when you put someone under intense pressure for too long, they make rash decisions to escape. Louise left while Dad was in hospital. I think in her mind, this was the best time to make the dash to the other side of the country, as Dad was being cared for and wasn't at risk. I was left at home with my stepbrother, whom I barely knew or spent time with as he spent most of his time at work or shut up in his room. I had $20 and no clue when Louise was coming home. I mainly lived off rice and soy sauce - possibly out of choice and possibly out of necessity. Luckily, it was the school holidays, so I could just focus on trying to look after Dad. I worked out I could afford to catch a bus to the hospital every other day to visit him. He was depressed and unsure of his future regarding his health, not to mention the adventures of his 'gypsy' wife.

It was a tough two weeks, but one thing I remember doing was praying. It was honestly the only thing that made sense and that I knew I could do. I would get up in the morning after my stepbrother left for work and prayed, crying out to God for help. I prayed for Dad to get better, and I prayed for my entire family to know the love of God the way I was learning to. Prayer was now a tool that I was using to stand upright and trust that this storm would pass.

I became very thankful for the diligence of Val back in Sale. She taught me about the love of God and showed me how to pray and focus on His Word. I wasn't scared, I was just focused on the two things I knew I could do - prayer and keep visiting Dad. I remember feeling pressure to help Dad, but there was nothing I could do but visit and bring him fresh clothing. The sense of responsibility left me feeling guilty as I had no means of fixing or improving the situation. My other siblings were not around, and I very much doubt they understood the magnitude of what was going on. They were young adults living their own lives, and they no longer felt any responsibility for their childhood home and family life. Louise had not informed them of Dad's declining situation and her spontaneous trip to Western Australia.

Louise returned after two weeks. Dad was home, still recovering, but he continued to have TIA's at home (a TIA is a medical acronym for Transient Ischaemic Attack - and it is a temporary blockage of blood flow to the brain that causes stroke-like symptoms). Dad was constantly stressed and could not talk about past pain from his previous marriage to Mum, or even about his childhood. He couldn't adjust to a new type of family, and his conflict with Louise's son couldn't be resolved. The decision was made. We were moving to Western Australia. New beginnings, new environment, and away from complicated family relationships.

For me, it felt like I was moving to a different planet. No longer would it be a two-hour train trip to visit my friends in Gippsland; it would now be a full four-hour flight plus a three-hour train ride at best! I was only sixteen and leaving home wasn't a viable option, so their decision to move across the country obviously had to include me moving with them.

At this stage, my relationship with school was on the rocks. It was a long-standing relationship that, well, to be frank, I was never really committed to. We tried, but we had totally different expectations of what we wanted out of relationship. School wanted me to keep up good grades to represent the image of the school well. Due to all the distractions at home, my grades went from a B average to a C or D average. I was finishing year ten when I decided to break up with my high school.

My eyes were set on finding a chef's apprenticeship. When I asked Dad if I could leave school, he was surprisingly supportive.

"As long as you do something, you're not just sitting at home." I already had my exit plan ready when I finally had the courage to ask if I could leave school. Dad knew that school and I were not a compatible couple, so I think he recognised at this stage it was not worth fighting to keep me in school.

I had time to start my apprenticeship through TAFE and finish my first term before we scooted over to the other side of the country.

I enjoyed TAFE, and I had great teachers who genuinely loved their trade. The other students were easy to get along with. I was still terrified of making mistakes or asking for help, so I often waited for others to make mistakes like slicing a finger open, burning a hand on a baking tray, or getting an order wrong when we did restaurant work. Chef apprenticeships were mainly full of young cocky lads, so to learn from other people's mistakes was a safe strategy.

I remember in my first year when we learned how to sharpen our knives. A few of the boys went out on their lunch break and smoked a joint, returning to class stoned out of their barely fully developed brains. Nevertheless, they proceeded to attempt to sharpen their knives on steel. One young lad's knife slipped and cut down between his thumb and pointer finger. He hit a tendon, and that was the end of his chef's career. I felt sorry for him because he was desperately trying to fit in with the group of boys who were clearly the head of the pack. Lesson one: Drugs are bad and compromise your ability to do simple tasks. Lesson two: Boys in a pack can make dumb decisions. Lesson three: I now knew how to sharpen my knives and to do so without significant injuries.

While in Western Australia, as I was finishing my apprenticeship, I was also working part-time at McDonald's. I had also found a small church that was a genuine blessing to me. I was content but firmly focused on returning to Victoria. I approached Dad right at the beginning of the move and asked him when I could leave home. He told me to give Western Australia twelve months, then, if I still felt the same, I would be able to leave and return to Sale where I felt my home truly was. With that promise set in my mind, everything I did during that time was all part of my countdown 'till the day I could move back home.

The little church I found was like a compass for me. It was a new church, pastored by a young couple. This little community of about twenty people demonstrated healthy relationships. Sound teaching of the Word of God kept me growing in my faith and feeding my curiosity about who God was. Home life wasn't crazy and chaotic anymore. I had created my own rhythm of living - church, work, and TAFE. We also lived near native bushland, so I often passed the time by exploring the bushland.

I was only sixteen, so I didn't have my driver's license yet, and I wasn't willing to ask Dad to teach me to drive due to his stress levels. I was doing my best to minimise stress for him and considering the fact that I crashed his car when we were still living in Victoria (writing it off the week I got my learner's permit), I figured driving wasn't a skill I was ready to learn yet anyway. I often worked the late shift, but instead of getting my parents to pick me up, as it was "my choice to work late," I would pay for a taxi. I was self-sufficient and independent during this time.

The stress of school was well and truly in the past. However, although Dad and Louise had distanced themselves from the issues of family, the internal dynamics in each of them were still at work. Dad was obviously depressed. The shock of not being able to return to work had crushed him. His ability to provide for his family and his very identity were intertwined in his career. His only family were his children, and three of them were on the other side of the country now. The TIA's continued to happen, and Dad became a shell of the man he once was. When a TIA happened, which was almost weekly at one stage, Dad would not tell anyone and simply take himself off to his bedroom to 'sleep it off.' The veins in his arms collapsed due to all the blood tests and the blood thinners he was on. Dad never spoke about how he was feeling within himself to his doctors. Addressing his emotional state was off limits to anyone trying to help. Louise was struggling to find work, and the reality of Dad's poor health was also taking its toll on her.

After twelve months had passed (to the day), I approached Dad about moving back home to Sale. I remember his face, seeing the sadness and loneliness of his last child leaving the nest etched into his eyes. But he was a man of his word, and true to his promise he gave me his blessing to leave. This was very hard as I felt a deep sense of guilt leaving Dad, knowing that he was struggling, and knowing he was lonely, but at the same time, I knew I had to leave. There were no more opportunities for me to grow at home. I felt very strongly about moving back to Gippsland, and I believed that moving back to my original church was where the next adventure was meant to begin.

Chapter 13

Grow Where You're Planted

Whilst living in Melbourne and in Western Australia, I had developed stronger friendships with my childhood friends from my church back in Sale. I tried to visit during school holidays and mostly stayed with one family, the Coffey's. They had two daughters and a son, all younger than me, and they had become some of my closest friends - basically like family. As young teenagers, we had been conspiring for years that when I eventually moved back to Sale, I would move into their home! When the time came for me to ask Dad if I could move back to Gippsland, I also asked Mr. and Mrs. Coffey, Michael and Yvonne, if I could live with them for a time when I moved back. I was petrified that they would say no and I would be left to fend for myself. Yvonne's response was, "Of course you can move in, we've always said we would have you stay."

In January 2000, it was hard to leave my parents' home. I was seventeen, and Dad, being a man who did not give much physical contact, surprised me by hugging me tightly at the airport. It was a hug from a father who was not truly ready to let his child go, yet he did. I was so thankful he stayed true to his word and that he released me into the wild, blue yonder. However, the look on his face is forever etched into my mind. It was sorrowful. Dad had a deep love for his children; even though he did not express it well; his whole world was his children. Unfortunately, Dad was not able to convey this love to us, so the relationship became distant over the years after we all moved out. Perhaps because I was the youngest and maybe because my Dad was all I knew as a parent, I witnessed firsthand his anguish and desire for a more meaningful relationship with us, his children.

I made every effort to call Dad regularly after moving out of home. I didn't get to see him for nearly eighteen months, as I could not afford to travel back to Western Australia to visit. I called Dad once a week, and his tone was always flat. He was usually quite negative about his situation, and I sensed that he felt rejected by his own children. Most times I called, Dad would ask me if I had heard from my siblings and if I knew what they were up to. They didn't contact Dad very often, simply because they were all in their 20's, in relationships, and were living and establishing their own lives. And even though I knew I couldn't take away the cloud of depression that covered Dad, I carried a great amount of sadness for him, mixed with a feeling of guilt that somehow I had contributed to the heaviness he was constantly under.

Life at the Coffey's was a dynamic change from the chaos of my dysfunctional family. It was like moving to a whole new planet. The family culture was not what I was used to. It was a sort of new form of chaos. There was communication between siblings and parents. Two parents who loved each other. And there were siblings that shared rooms and argued and then resumed playing whatever game it was that had caused the fight in the first place.

Family discussions were common, especially when there were disagreements - any issues that arose could be resolved. It was fantastic! I went from entertaining myself and looking after what needed to be looked after in the home without being told to, to discussions about who did the dishes last and why a certain sibling always needed to go to the toilet when the clean up after dinner needed to happen. I shared a room with sisters, Phoebe and Sarah. This was a real circus most of the time. Poor Sarah, who was twelve at the time, suffered from asthma and needed a nebuliser most nights (which is a machine that helps with the intake of asthma medication through an oxygen mask). We often fell asleep to the sound of the gentle murmur of this machine. Other nights, Sarah liked to fall asleep listening to an audio book - Trixie Belden was her favourite. Quiet was no longer a normal part of my surroundings.

The politics of the room boundaries grew intense between the three teenage girls. We all decided that making clear boundaries was the best solution. In the room was one single bed and a set of bunk beds, which Sarah and I shared. Sarah suggested sticky tape down the middle of the room, which also divided the doorway, as a good place to start. Yet instead of going all the way to the other side, the tape stopped halfway, and another line was placed horizontally. This ensured that Sarah had the desk and the window in her boundary area, and Phoebe and I had the doorway. We felt it was fair to give Sarah what she preferred, as she was in the top bunk.

We thought our act of sacrifice and maturity would justify our next move. Of course, our motives weren't that pure. Sarah's boundary did not permit her to enter or exit through the door, so we enforced the rule that Sarah was only allowed to climb through the window to get in and out of the room, which included going to the bathroom at night. I was no longer the youngest child!

It was a lively house, to say the least. I was now a part of a family that was functional and involved in a church whose passion was to serve the community. There were a lot of young people who were a part of the youth group connected to the church. To the best of our ability, we spent every waking moment hanging out together. We organised car washes, working bees, as well as getting up to borderline-risky antics! There was so much life in our friendships, and with all of us between fourteen to mid-twenties, there was a lot of energy and hope for the future.

Michael and Yvonne Coffey ©

Our pastors, Brian and Lynne, had a defined passion for people and connecting them to the love of God. This vision is still very much the culture of the church today. Our pastors would pour hours every week into the young people, whether it was through Bible studies, dinners at their house which often turned into late night hangouts, playing games, playing music, and talking about the power of God's love.

My pastors also had a young family of six children, all of whom were part of my close friendship circle. They were dedicated to both their family and following the call of God on their lives, which for them meant leading a church and mentoring around twenty misfit, wayward youth. To me, Pastor Brian and Lynne were by no means a replacement for my own family, but they were a different type of family or relationship that enabled me to understand and personally know God for myself. They were way makers, exposing a clear pathway forward. I personally looked at them as two individuals and recognised an inspirational man and woman who were determined to build a life together that, first and foremost, put God above everything.

Pastor Lynne was, and still is, a remarkable woman. She is humble, yet incredibly strong. She has always been consistent in how she relates to everyone, which for me meant safety. She's creative and resourceful, and an extra person (or ten) at dinnertime did not faze her a bit. Even though they did not have a big income, no one would have felt the financial strain they might have been under. Their love for people was far greater than the fear of being broke. Pastor Lynne has always been a no-nonsense, matter of fact woman who is never moved by the emotional mood swings of teenagers and young adults. At the same time, she's a woman who is full of joy and has always encouraged us to have fun and to be creative. She was the second stable matriarch (after Val) to influence my life.

Me with Pastors Brian and Lynne Heath from Sale ©

Pastor Brian has always been passionate about his love for God and ensuring that others have the opportunity to know God personally, as well as grow in their personal understanding of who He is. He understands the value of Scripture and encouraged all the youth to memorise passages in the Bible. Pastor Brian knew that when the pressure of life hit us, only the word of God, paired with the Holy Spirit, was going to sustain us and cause us to grow through trials and tribulation. He has always been a visionary - someone who is never comfortable with the status quo or staying as you are and forever learning how to push through personal barriers to move towards the goal set before you. I think this ability of Pastor Brian to establish vision, unlocked something in me. I could see myself as someone who was always envisioning the future and working towards something far greater than myself.

At twenty-one now, here I was back in my hometown of Sale, living with a family whose children were two of my best friends, going to church, and living life. I was working flat out at two jobs and saving hard because I wanted to buy my own house. I was begging to learn how to listen to God's will and to be obedient, especially when things seemed impossible. I was ready to move out of the Coffey's house and spread my wings, but the idea of renting seemed silly. Why pay someone else's mortgage instead of my own? Honestly, it was that simple for me. Working in hospitality does not pay well. I had no idea how I would afford the repayments, but my focus was on getting a deposit and then figuring out the rest, trusting that God had inspired me to take this next step and follow His lead.

Then the proverbial storm hit. Ps Brian hit burnout. He was completely incapacitated both physically and emotionally. For around three months, we did not see him. Both Pastor Brian and Lynne lay low to recover from years of pushing themselves hard - to lead a church and raise a family and work full-time. They gave themselves fully to everyone around them. This was terrifying. These two people were so precious to me, and the thought of them suffering and struggling broke our hearts.

As a church, we wanted to look after them and care for them, so it was suggested by other members of the church who were close to Pastor Brian and Lynne, to help them buy their own house. They had always rented, never being able to have their own home due to the financial sacrifice they'd made by choosing to lead a church over building a career. As soon as the opportunity arose to give money towards their house deposit, I clearly knew what I wanted to do. I was only twenty-one, no one spoke to me directly, and there was no expectation or pressure from anyone to give money towards their dream home. I was not exactly stashing wads of cash under my mattress. I was barely an adult who boarded with a family and worked in hospitality I looked at my bank account, and the debate in my head began. I only had 5,000 dollars, but that was the equivalent of one million for a twenty-one-year-old. I believed strongly that I should give all of what was in my account ... then the negotiations in my head kicked in. "What about half, then you still have a chance of working on your own deposit?" "If you give it all, you will be living with the Coffeys forever!" "There is no way you can make back what you give, you don't earn enough".

Then the most rational thought entered my head, "Why would you not trust God? You don't negotiate with God, He's God!" To put it frankly, I snapped out of the debate when I realised - if I truly believed in God, the God who created the heavens and the earth, the God who delivered the Israelites out of slavery, the God who raised Jesus from the dead, then I could not compromise on what I believed He was asking me to do. I emptied my account, placed a wad of cash in an envelope, and gave it to the person in our church who was going to pass on our contributions to Pastor Brian and Lynne. I felt euphoric – which is what happens when you let go of what you thought was so important. I kept thinking, "It's just money. How great is it going to be to see Pastor Brian and Lynne in their own home!" My focus had completely changed from fear of not having enough for myself, to excitement about the possibilities for pastor Brian and Lynne and how God was going to bless them.

Our pastors finally had a deposit for a house! Other finances had come through for them, real estate prices were at an all-time low, and within six weeks of giving towards this amazing dream, they had purchased their very own home in one of the nicest areas in Sale. It was an amazing time watching what God can do with what seemed like an impossible situation. Pastor Brian was beginning to recover from burnout and beauty was being formed from the ashes.

Chapter 14

Giving Makes The Way

I hadn't lost hope of buying my own house, but there's no denying it was hard to save another deposit. I worked as much as I could, took up babysitting jobs, and I would take any random cash-in-hand work that was offered to me. I became the queen of turning up at people's houses just to say hi, at around 6 pm, of course. When they offered me dinner, I would not want to offend my friends and was obliged to have a free meal - I was savvy with my ability to save! Slowly, slowly, I saved everything I could. I did not lose sight of the possibility of owning my own house, but in reality, that's all it was - a possibility.

I had no plan or real understanding of how to purchase a house. I simply knew that if I had no deposit, I could kiss the dream goodbye. I was learning one of the most vital lessons during this time – to align myself with the Father's will and He would go before me. Being obedient by giving my hard earned cash towards Pastor Brian and Lynne's home, which I believed was an instruction from God, did two things: it positioned me to believe and know that God is far greater than any financial issue, and it allowed God to give me more than I expected because I was now learning to look up towards heaven instead of out towards the impossible.

I became bold and started making appointments with real estate agents to look through houses on the market. Everything I looked at was out of my price range, but I was beginning to dream more and more. And to be honest, it was sort of fun looking through other people's homes and seeing what they had done with their little pocket of paradise.

A short time later, a real estate agent called me. He explained that there was a house I should look at in my price bracket - but I needed to be open-minded. Which was clearly code for "if you don't open your eyes, it's perfect in every way."

Arriving at the house, which was right on the cusp of the questionable edge of town, I noticed most of the houses in the street were privately owned, which was a good start. The street was home to old Defence Force housing built in the 80's. (I'd like to say at this point, housing provided for the Defence has changed dramatically since then.) It was a little three-bedroom house with a tiny kitchen, one bathroom, and an outside laundry. The house was currently rented, and it turned out that I knew the boys who were renting it! As I walked through the house into the first bedroom, the 'styling' of the room grabbed my attention. Slip Knot posters were on the walls, and prized bongs were displayed on the windowsill. "Be open-minded, be open-minded" was on repeat in my head.

When I returned to the lounge room, I began to see the potential, and I started to get excited. The other thought that I continually focused on was, "This is not your forever home, it's just the first step." We finished the inspection, and I promptly asked for a second inspection so that I could bring a more qualified adult with me to view the property. Yvonne and Michael came with me and encouraged me to investigate purchasing the property. They too must have squinted to see the potential as a young woman's home rather than a lad's den.

I felt like I was following steppingstones, not knowing what the process of buying a house entailed. But everything was lining up, and my bank manager was an amazing gentleman who was on my side.

Our government had just announced the first homeowner grant, and I was able to access this together with the minimum deposit required. Things were progressing quickly. I had just over $5,000 in my bank account, and this was the exact amount I needed to purchase the house. The exact amount that I had given was the exact amount that was required. I needed to have my finances approved before I could make an offer, so the application process for a home loan began. It only took a week for the bank to do whatever they had to do, which I'm sure is just by popping numbers into their computer and pressing a magic button, before they contacted me to tell me I had been approved for a home loan! Immediately, I called the real estate agent to make an offer. I offered below the asking price because apparently that's what you are meant to do. An hour later, the agent called me back with the news that the owner had accepted my offer!

What had just happened? My head was spinning with shock, excitement, and fear. Who would give a twenty-one-year-old, casually employed hospitality worker cash for a house? It seemed hilarious to me. This was just six months after giving all I had out of obedience to God. Now I was signing papers for my own home!

When the settlement date came around, I had plans to take out a wall that divided the kitchen and the lounge room and to polish the floorboards. I am forever thankful to my friends who helped me during this budget renovation because it really did make a derelict rental property into a home and a sanctuary. The wall removal cost me two bottles of wine, and the floors were a few hundred dollars plus a solid two weeks of work from my close friends. The bank account was dry, but I had a nest of my own!

One of my best friends was moving in with me. We had nothing to furnish the house with and no cash to buy anything. Well, that's not completely true - it was November, Christmas was in the air, and I was a first-time homeowner! My friend Yolanda and I went 'shopping', getting an early start to fantasy Christmas shopping. Neither of us had money to spend, and Yolanda was the same age as me, working in retail and about to start university. I had about $100 surplus cash in my account after bleeding it dry with the purchases for my house.

Yolanda and I wandered into the Christmas display area at Myer, and I became fixated on the most perfect of Christmas trees. I wanted it and I needed it. Close to $200, I was not getting it unless Yolanda also invested in my plastic dream tree! I begged, I bargained, and finally, Yolanda knew what the right decision was to make. We came up with a fair deal.

She would pay half now, but when she eventually moved out, the dream tree was hers. Deal! Nothing like immediate gratification! The tree was mine, sort of! A week later, I moved into my first home. Polished floorboards, an open living area, and one of my best gal pals! The move was fast and easy, considering all I had was a Christmas tree. Yolanda and I set up the dream tree, and we sat on the floor looking at the best purchase of our adult lives. A shimmering, shining beacon of joy. There was a conversation during this time that we probably should have gotten bean bags instead of the tree, but then we came to our senses...bean bags would be a bad investment as they are only temporary. They're a waste of money, yet a dream tree would last forever - logically, still a better investment.

I was camping in my room for a week when my brother, Rod, who was now working for his father-in-law's removalist company, called me up to see if I needed anything for my house. The words "literally everything" sprang out of my mouth. Big Brother came to the rescue. He told me that it wasn't uncommon for people to leave things behind when they move. Rod arrived at my house a few days later with a couch, a washing machine, a small table and chairs, and a bed! Luckily, we didn't get beanbags! Other people gave me super practical housewarming presents, and it wasn't long before my house really did have the appeal of a home.

Renting the rooms to friends was an easy solution to keep up with the mortgage repayments, and at the age of twenty-one it was fun to live with close friends. I loved having people over for dinner. I had deliberately determined to create a home environment so that whoever walked into my home felt at ease and safe from whatever else was going on in their world. Whether people were at my house hanging out or we all gathered at someone else's house, it's safe to say I was rarely alone at night.

My working life was busy, my social life was busy, and my church life was busy. The busyness was a deliberate attempt on my part to feel valued and to avoid the reality of the darkness that was constantly around me, even though I was establishing myself in a place where I believed I was meant to be. However, the deep-seated issues that I had built my identity on were a constant torment. Nevertheless, I was planted in the right place. This was the right place to challenge and change the very foundation of who I was.

Chapter 15

Working, It's What You're Good At

At twenty-one, I was living in a town I loved, I had fantastic friends, and I was working hard. But the first signs of depression were now becoming obvious to others. However, I was in deep denial due to the feeling of shame attached to the belief and fear of failing. One of my friends flagged his concerns, asking me if I thought I had depression. His question was like a royal slap in the face. I was working hard to keep it together, and I truly believed no one could see how much I was struggling. I also believed that my greatest attribute was my ability to work and my capacity to keep going. I felt useful and valued when I felt I could offer more of my time to help others. Whether it was working longer hours to be approved by my employer or saying yes and making myself available to be there for a friend, or to help at church... this was what I was good at, and I did not feel that I had anything else to offer. I refused to ask for help and felt a sense of pride when people came to me for help. If people offered to help, I would take this to mean I was incompetent.

I looked at others around me and saw intelligent, smart, attractive people who had far better abilities than me. I measured my success by my capacity to work hard. I committed to everything to feel a sense of approval and a sense of love from others. The brokenhearted child who was left in the care of a nanny was now an adult and still believed that she was not worthy of love. I was scared of becoming truly close to people for fear they would be disappointed and angry with all my flaws.

One day, when my friend asked this pivotal question, "Do you think you have depression?" it evoked a double-edged response in me - shame of exposure, and relief that someone could see my struggle. How could they see my inward struggle? After that conversation, I made a promise to go and talk to someone. I decided to approach my pastors about what was going on but could not explain in any real detail why I was feeling so depressed. I couldn't find the words, unless you include crying as a language. I was ashamed of some of the thoughts that were constantly circling around in my head and didn't yet dare to be honest about the deep-seated pain I was experiencing. My pastors strongly suggested going to a GP for guided support, so I made the appointment and committed to getting medical insight. I was terrified of fronting up to a doctor's clinic. The thought of admitting I was struggling was one thing, but I knew that they would ask me questions about my family history. In the back of my head were fears of following in my mother's footsteps. The appointment was brief and painful.

The GP confirmed that I was suffering from depression. So, they prescribed me antidepressant medication and informed me that the medication might be something I would have to use for the rest of my life, given the family history. No other suggestions for managing depression were offered, and I was given no explanation about what depression was. I was now labelled another statistic with mental health issues; I was officially broken. The doctor gave me no indication that I would get better and suggested going to a counsellor, which I could not afford. I was not ready to talk to anyone, and I was offered no other suggestions to help me out of this hole.

I had felt this heaviness for years and accepted that this was a part of who I was. I was confused, rejected, and without a real purpose. I loved my church, my friends, and my disjointed family, but still felt disconnected and unworthy of receiving any form of love.

The thoughts of confusion around sexuality, thoughts of being unworthy, and thoughts of suicide constantly flooded my thinking. These ideas felt like they had their own persona, trying to sell me what they had to offer as the solution to freedom. Keeping busy and trying to create a sense of worth by working hard became my solution to keeping depression at bay.

Dream Loud

Though the struggle in me was a constant raging war, I also had a deep-seated passion to help people. Even in high school, when I was volunteering for Kids Help Line and Amnesty International, I found deep fulfilment in advocating for and helping others. I was able to express this passion through my church in many ways. Kids programs, youth mentoring in local schools, helping local businesses, and helping maintain the street decorations. We also organised working bees for people who needed a helping hand. The heart of our church has always been to show the love of God through serving, which brought me so much joy. My pastors have always encouraged me to dream big to bring the love of God to people.

Dreaming was never an issue for me, but having the confidence to share my dreams was a big problem. What if people don't agree with the vision? What if they ask questions that I don't have the answers to? How on earth could I achieve anything I'm dreaming of?

In 2006, (I was twenty-four), a group of friends and I from church went on a trip to Malaysia for an international youth conference run by a church in Malaysia. It was an amazing time, travelling with friends, making new friends from all over the world, and staying up all night eating random Asian food while building new friendships.

The conference had some workshop sessions, from music to leadership-related topics. I put my name down for a 'Dream Builder' workshop. I didn't know what I was getting myself into, but I just had this strong feeling that I needed to be in this workshop. The presenter was a man named JR. He was from America, and his wife was from China, and they had set up an organisation in China aimed at rescuing children off the streets. They housed them and gave them a good education to break the cycle of poverty. They were inspiring. I don't remember the details of the session that JR ran, but from start to finish I was inspired, even during the part where I wanted to vanish and not be seen. We were asked to do an activity where we would write down what our dreams were with "I am" statements, like "I am the owner of a Ferrari". The idea was to stop looking at vision as a wish list, but rather as something attainable that you are responsible for. I had never told anyone what my dreams were, ever. Fear always stopped me. Yet in that moment, I committed to being bold and dreaming big. I wrote down ten "I am" statements, including "I am running my own cafe, which has a safe and caring environment for young people." "I am training young people in hospitality in a healthy environment". "I am living in a home that is a home to others where they can begin to heal and come alive again".

Writing these things down was a massive achievement. I was acknowledging the dreams that were deep inside of me, even while doubting the possibility of seeing them come to life. I was not prepared for the next task either. "Now read them out to the person next to you," said JR. Are you kidding me? This is the biggest risk ever on the face of the earth! Being exposed! You don't expose yourself; the risk of getting hurt is too high. Strangely enough, none of my friends were with me in this workshop; it was just me and twenty other strangers. I knew if I backed out of this part, I was going to let fear win. My thoughts were, "You'll never see any of these people again; if they criticise your dreams, no one back home will ever know." Next to me was the sweetest girl who was only a few years younger than me. We chatted for a minute before we launched into reading out our dreams. As she read hers first, I began to realise the significance of sharing with another person. I was feeling excited for her and wanted to hear more about her dreams, more details of what she saw.

My turn came, and as I read my dreams out, a few tears left my eyes out of relief and thankfulness that I hadn't run from this challenge. My new friend was encouraging but looked slightly confused as to why I was crying. I told her that this was the first time I'd ever shared my dreams with anyone. After that moment, I determined to continue to write down my "I am" statements every day, which I did for six months.

(I was not going to include this last part in my story because firstly I had forgotten about it, but as I was writing this memory came back to me, and I realised the significance of speaking out your dreams. It's one thing to keep vision and dreams in your head, but until it is spoken out, it can never physically come to pass.)

We returned from the youth conference pumped up after being in such an inspirational environment and meeting so many great people from around the world. I began talking to one of my close friends about my vision of opening my own cafe - a cafe that sets a different standard for hospitality. A place that genuinely cared for the staff and the customers. A place where we taught young people essential skills, as well as showing them a different standard of relating to each other. I wanted to build a business that was an extension of our church culture. The more I talked about this vision, the more I was convinced it was a good idea and began to feel more and more compelled to take the risk of starting my own business.

My friend also became convinced that this was a challenge worth taking on, so we approached our pastors to hear what they thought of two young women building a business together. Our pastors loved the vision, but from their vantage point, they knew that this was a massive challenge to embark upon. I was working three jobs and knew there was no more future in hospitality for me, but with a mortgage and no other financial backing, no bank was going to look at me for a loan. My friend was working in a good job and had secure employment, but she too had a mortgage and couldn't get a loan for our venture. We kept looking at possible locations and trying to convince our banks to give us loans, but door after door kept shutting.

I'm a fairly glass-half-full type of person - coming up against a wall just means you must look for a way around it, but this situation looked impossible. Then we were approached by a couple in our church. I'm not sure how they heard of what we were wanting to do, but they came and offered to loan us the money for setting up the cafe! This was huge. Not only was the dream becoming a reality, but others believed in the dream.

At the same time, a little cafe in town was selling; it needed a lot of love, but I could see all the potential trapped underneath the seven-year buildup of grease on the kitchen walls. We made an offer, they accepted, and things were in motion. The vision was getting legs and was about to run. Our crazy plan was that I would quit my jobs and run the cafe, while my business partner would look after the books and finances. We wanted to put a small amount of money into freshening up the cafe and changing the layout. We also needed some equipment and new signage for the front. So, as soon as we had the keys to our brand new, fresh out of the womb business baby, we went to work to transform the space. I calculated that I only had two weeks between resigning and needing to start earning an income. So, two weeks was our timeline to refresh this tired space. The mind and energy of a 25-year-old! Our friends all came to chip in on the work that needed to be done. We worked back into the early hours of the morning just because we knew time was so limited. We made it through those two weeks with a lot of problem-solving and no real setbacks, but the learning had begun. And there it was - a brand-new cafe in the centre of town. Tall Poppy Cafe was born!

I remember the opening vividly, as I was petrified that first day. I'd worked in hospitality since I'd left school, but now, I was representing my own business. People knew that I was part of a church, so I was representing our church too, so the pressure was huge. The fear of what others were thinking and that I may not deliver what people were expecting plagued my mind as we opened the door for the first time. Thankfully, we were very busy from the moment we opened the door, so I simply didn't have time to entertain my thoughts for too long. The first day and the first weeks were exhausting to say the least, but extremely exciting. We were off to a great start. We had a good team of workers, some of whom stayed with us through the whole journey of the business.

One of my best friends, Beck, came to work with us as she was as excited about the vision of the business as we were. Within moments of starting work with us, she came to me with a vision of a cooking school for primary school-aged children. I loved the idea and soon 'Little Chef Academy' was born. We were running a business within a business. The Academy started at 4 pm, so we would close the cafe, clean and set it up for students to come, then pack up after the cooking school. We did this three days a week. We had also expanded into catering through the cafe side of the business, and while Little Chefs was taking off, we were getting asked to do kids' parties. A lot was happening, and I genuinely loved what the cafe was bringing to our town.

Unfortunately, my business partner didn't share the same vision for what we were doing, and the reality of the work behind the operation was, I think, overwhelming for her. With all that work, we were barely making ends meet financially. Often, there were weeks when I would not receive a wage, which was my choice. My solution for my lack of income was to start another business outside of cafe hours. I decided to train to become a personal trainer. (Somehow, outside of work, I attended a gym and discovered a new interest in fitness. Looking back, the gym was my outlet for the stress that I was under and just didn't realise it.) I qualified as a personal trainer and started a new business. I ran boot camps, group training, and did one-on-one training with clients. At one point, I was running a training program with another trainer for a local football team!

I would fit this in before the cafe opened and, in the evening, after closing for the night. The good thing was that the money I was making took some of the pressure off the cafe.

My business partner and I were managing to maintain the cafe to the best of our ability. We would have our struggles, but we managed to keep on going. She was probably thinking, "This is not what I signed up for." I was thinking, "I just want a business partner who can see the vision and potential of what we are doing." I know in some ways she did see parts of the bigger picture. She was incredibly encouraging to me as the business grew and we were making a name for ourselves within the Sale community. I didn't feel I could talk to anyone about what was going on. I felt immense responsibility for the financial situation of the business and felt responsible for the pressure that my business partner was feeling. She was one of my best friends, and I valued our friendship greatly.

Chapter 16

Help!

I felt dead inside. I had learned to protect myself from rejection by assuming that people would hurt me either intentionally or unintentionally. I wanted to be loved and feel the power of connection to others, but instead, fear ruled my decision making. To admit I was struggling or that I didn't have the answers to the issues I was facing would be like disqualifying myself from being loved. People love people who are capable and functional. Right? I clung to my work ethic and endurance as a way of "winning" the approval of others. This was also the way I won God's approval. My mind was a mess. Maybe God would overlook how much I had failed within myself if I served him well. The only problem was that what I believed was serving God was actually slavery to my shame. I chose to maintain these beliefs, and by choosing to believe the lies about who I was and how others saw me, I was continually turning my back on God. I was choosing death over life.

At twenty-eight years of age, I faced a crossroads. I worked 70-80 hours a week, running two businesses, managing staff, caring for customers/clients, and ensuring the operations of the café functioned while still trying to maintain a social life, living with housemates, and helping out at church in any way possible. My mind was in overdrive - I was lucky if I got three hours' sleep a night. I was burned out and running from God who wanted to save me.

The shadows were becoming darker and darker. The narrative in my head was a constant echo of failure and comparison. I had failed the people around me who had invested in my vision. I had failed the community I loved. I desperately wanted to contribute positively to my community but felt I was gradually letting people down. I compared myself to others who I believed had it all together and were successful, regardless of the pressure around them.

My family was horribly disconnected. Dad was battling his way through my step mum's mental health issues. She had recently been diagnosed with bipolar disorder, and I was trying to support dad through it as best I could. I would visit them as often as possible to give Dad a break from Louise or to give Louise a break from Dad.

I was struggling with my very identity. Maybe all this was not working because I was someone else and living a lie. Was I gay? Was I transgender? Why didn't I belong? The more I tried to find answers, the darker it became. Shame caused me to move my heart further and further away from God. The seeds of inaccurate ideas and thoughts from my eight-year-old self had never been weeded out; had never even been noticed. Conditions were now perfect for them to grow and bloom.

Moments were rare that I would feel happy and content; and then it would only last for a second. Audible thoughts would quickly invade and terminate those moments. "You know this won't last. You know, people will see through you. You won't be able to keep up the act. You don't deserve to be happy. You should be ashamed. Dying will relieve the world of this mess you have created." I was convincing myself that not only were these thoughts true, but I was unworthy of love or care and was simply a burden to others. I had opened the gates for pure evil to enter my heart. Evil doesn't produce life, it takes it away.

I was heavily medicated on antidepressants, not able to feel any sense of warmth from another person. The evidence of failure was accumulating in my head, and I was losing the fight. I was stockpiling medication, knowing that I could exit this battlefield at any point. I was fighting with myself every day just to keep going. Finally, one night I was home alone. For the first time in a long time, I had no housemates living with me, and so, for the very first time I was left alone with my thoughts. The thoughts of failure were hammering me, like a loud megaphone screaming in my head. They cancelled every possible thought of hope and change.

All I could do was sob uncontrollably. I can't describe the volume of my crying; I was out of control and was about to make the fatal decision to end my life. One thing that kept coming into my mind was that my business partner had always said to message her at any time if I needed to. She was aware of my battle with depression. I privately made a deal that if I sent her a message and she didn't reply - that would be confirmation that suicide was the only option. It was late at night, around 11:30 pm, when I sent the message in utter fear. "She's going to know how pathetic I am, and how much I have failed." She responded almost immediately and assured me that she would come over right away. She must have freaked out when she pulled up to my house. She said she could hear me crying from the street, so she called Pastor Lynne and asked her to come around. I was inconsolable. Pastor Lynne asked what was wrong, and I simply blurted out, "I've failed!"

"Failed what?", she asked.

At this point, I had that cry going on that sounded like an asthma attack with a strobe effect, like you have to take a run up to the words you are trying to say.

"My b... b... busi... business, m... m... my fri... frien... friends annn ... and f.. f.. fam family. I... I... I... I've fai...led you guys." (Meaning my pastors whom I value incredibly.)

My pastor's response was perfect. She sat me down and held me in a proper mum-hug. Like a baby, I cried into her arms while she prayed, at times asking God's presence to come and fill my heart, and some moments we just sat in silence. We didn't talk about the details; we didn't talk about strategies to feel better, and there were no words of false hope. I was fighting off hell, there was no denying it, but for the first time I had taken a gigantic step in a very different direction – I had asked for help. I had rejected death and began to move towards life by daring to risk rejection so that someone could help me in my helplessness. This was the beginning of my "hell NO!" faze, which, to be frank, has never ended. I was learning that you are responsible for saying no to Hell, that cycles can end, and your mind, body, and spirit can all be retrained and renewed. The only requirements are responsibility and commitment to the process of change.

That night, I went to bed, still crying and battling the fear of not being able to sleep. I had never been able to sleep a solid eight hours in my life, but the fear of losing my mind from exhaustion was real. That night, I prayed and asked for forgiveness. "God, I'm so sorry. Please help me, help me sleep". I was handing over my pride for the first time and letting God be God. I was letting His Spirit truly come into my life.

I still had all the responsibilities and pressures around me, so a few weeks after this game-changing moment in my living room, I arrived at a church function one night, and I was completely unable to keep the mask on. Pastor Lynne approached me to see how I was, and I broke down. Again, I broke into pieces. "I'm so tired," I wept. Her response was exactly what was needed. "You're not going to work tomorrow."

Fear was all over me as I replied, "I have to, I can't shut the shop."

Confidently, she reassured me, "We'll look after it all."

The matriarch had spoken, and to this day I have no idea how my cafe kept going during this time. One of my friends took annual leave to help, and different people volunteered their time to fill shifts. Friends from church and outside of church all came to the rescue.

One of my closest friends moved in with me to make sure I was resting and wasn't going to do anything stupid. For six weeks I attempted to rest and catch my breath. But I was so wound up I could not sit still. I had no energy or ability to concentrate. At one point my friend confronted me and stated bluntly, "You don't know how to relax."

"I do, I am relaxing" I snapped back as I proceeded to detail-clean the cutlery draw. She shoved five dollars into my hand and told me to go for a drive and get a coffee somewhere. I did, out of defiance, to prove her wrong. Fifteen minutes down the road, as I was taking my 'carefree drive' to relax, I realised I'd been kicked out of my own house! In her defence I must have been driving her crazy.

During this time, I was determined and committed to break off the calcification that had grown around my heart. I knew I had to tackle my number one lie that was forever tormenting me and impacting my relationship with God and therefore my relationship with people. I needed to risk being rejected to overcome the fear of rejection. I started making regular appointments to see Pastor Lynne. We just went to a cafe or something, so nothing outrageous or crazy. I would send her a text message and then wait, expecting her to tell me she didn't have time. She was always willing and made time to catch up. Then on the days that we had agreed to meet up I would anticipate again that plans would be cancelled. They never were. It was a constant anxiety battle fuelled by fear. While we were spending time together, I would freeze up and forget how to speak proper English. Given that English is the only language I can speak, this presented quite the problem. I was so afraid of saying the wrong thing or looking stupid or fully exposing the mess that was occupying my heart. But every two weeks I committed to sending a message and doing war with the fear that was dominating my life. I didn't realise it at the time, but I was beginning to move into Gods presence. Instead of wanting to be perfect and control relationships and my environment, I was admitting helplessness and acknowledging that what I believed about myself and others was inaccurate and producing death within me.

Facing reality is the ultimate key. You can't build a house on a rubbish pile, but many people do and blame the collapse on everyone else. I was beginning to see what I had built my life on. What I thought I understood about myself was, well, wrong. There's no other fluffy way to put it. But at this point, I was beginning to grab hold of the understanding that things could be rebuilt, and life could be regained. I am responsible for the rebuild. Now of course, I didn't sign up for a dysfunctional family, and I didn't choose to be exposed to things no child should ever have to endure. To protect myself I had established patterns in my life - patterns to relate to others without getting hurt, patterns of how I saw myself that explained why people would leave me. I had learned these patterns from my childhood, and they had never been challenged; I had built them in response to my environment.

I never blamed anyone in my family for the events that took place; I blamed myself for not being better, for not being able to help more, for not being able to care for my parents and make things better. And when things fell apart, I felt I must have contributed to the implosion. However, I was no longer that six-year-old little girl; now I am twenty-eight and understand that change is possible, but I am responsible for moving into the light and exposing the darkness that was established around me. I was becoming aware of the possibility that I could attain freedom, and that life only comes when you let go of your patterns of doing things. When you let go of your established beliefs and you acknowledge your humanity, your weakness, then comes the opportunity to grow and become who you were created to be. Without the connection to others and the connection to the Giver of life, there is just work without any real fulfilment. How can you see God if you are not even facing Him? How can you be found in His presence if you don't respond to His voice and obey? Shame will make you walk towards the darkness, and arrogance will keep you there. God is good, and everything He has created is good, but when we try to build a 'good life' independently, we think that we can do what only God can do, which is to give life. So, who then are we receiving life from?

God shows us His mercy and His willingness to strengthen us and to rebuild us when we are overwhelmed by shame. He doesn't require us to first complete our mission for Him before

He approves of us. He simply wants us—as we are—so He can work in and through us:

2 Corinthians 12:10 (NJKV), *'For when I am weak, then I am strong.'* We find fulfilment in His presence because we are part of Him. Through all of this I felt like I was breaking, but in actual fact I was coming to a point of truly knowing God and becoming an open vessel for His Spirit to restore me.

Chapter 17

Turning Point

Returning to work at the cafe was different now. I was still working hard but began to make small adjustments to reduce my days from six to five days a week. I could feel that there was a change in the air, but I was very unsure what this would look like. I continued to maintain the business for as long as I needed to. Six years into running Tall Poppy Cafe, my business partner and I began to talk about selling. She was ready to move on. I was still struggling to see what my next step was. I didn't want to go back into hospitality working for someone else, as I was afraid of never getting out of hospitality and always struggling financially. When we sold, I needed a new vision, a new plan.

I was still maintaining my second business as a personal trainer during this time. One day, when I was training a group of women, I was feeling bored listening to them talk about all their problems at home and with their partners. I was bored because I wanted to make people lift weights and push themselves, not listen to them drone on about their problems. Then I realised that these women didn't need a personal trainer for fitness, they needed a personal trainer for their personal lives! They needed the adjustment that I was going through! Back in the cafe, I started to look at my customers and noticed that the regulars were regular because Tall Poppy Cafe was their refuge.

For nearly seven years, we had been a place for many to escape for just a moment from the pain and chaos of whatever they were going through. I had sat with customers who needed to talk about the stress of parenting. I had walked with one customer while she grieved over the sudden loss of her husband. I had heard countless stories of elderly people missing their spouses who had passed away or children who lived too far away. I had taught countless children the joy of cooking and what cross-contamination was. I was a good listener, but more so, I now wanted people to heal and feel life the way I was beginning to, through God Himself.

I began to consider a complete career change; a genuine risk of going to university to become a counsellor. I prayed and prayed - not about potentially going to university, but I prayed constantly for the people around me. "God help them to know your love. God help me to show them how awesome you are." While praying, I would often find myself daydreaming about helping young people who were forgotten and completely messed up. Taking them camping, teaching them skills while listening to their stories of brokenness. My desire to help people was beginning to take a different form.

Talking with my pastors about the idea of going to university and studying to be a counsellor was met with encouragement. I shared my thoughts about wanting to help people and felt that there was not enough support out there to help people struggling. And, let's be honest, some of the qualified people in the counselling industry were a little mental themselves. By opening my mouth and sharing my new dream meant that I was now daring to tackle one of my biggest false beliefs about myself, the very reason I dropped out of high school - the belief that I was stupid and incompetent at learning.

The crossroad was right there in front of me. Keep nurturing the fear of failing and stay in hospitality or take the risk, try something new and see what happens.

One morning in the cafe, I shared my idea of going to university with one of my regular customers. She was an older woman in her sixties. She had lived a good life and had a very interesting career in corporate management. She was a good listener, kind-hearted, and a matter-of-fact type of woman. I enjoyed many conversations with her over the years. I spoke to her about my fears of going to university and how I worried about what people would think if I failed at it. She made one comment that put everything into perspective.

"Well Jo, how old will you be when you graduate?"

"I'll be thirty-five."

"Well, you're going to turn thirty-five with a piece of paper or without it; either way you're going to turn thirty-five. It's up to you what you want that to look like."

I really don't believe she knew how profound her words were. Time is going to go by, we can't control that, but what we do with the time we've been given is our responsibility. If fear was the only thing stopping me, it wasn't a justifiable reason to not try.

By the end of that week, I had submitted my application to university, which I discovered wasn't that hard. Three weeks later I received the email that would catapult me into a new season of my life, a new season of challenge and growth. I opened the email in the privacy of my room in case I was about to be rejected; I wasn't. I was accepted into university! My self-esteem was so incredibly low that I was genuinely shocked and burst into tears. I thanked God repeatedly as I cried. New doors were opening, and this confirmed in my heart that selling my beloved business was now officially an easy decision.

I struggled with the idea of selling the business for a short while, not because it was my business and I had made a name for myself through it, but because I felt a sense of responsibility to keep running the cafe as it served so many people within the community. But I was well over the work and the physical commitment of running a business.

One customer broke my heart when I sat down and told her I was selling the business. She cried into her coffee and looked at me and said, "What am I going to do?" This beautiful woman had come to Tall Poppy Cafe every Thursday for years. She started coming with her husband and I would sit down with them and hear about their children and their marriage. I watched as her husband succumbed to Alzheimer's and he gradually became a very vacant man. Eventually he went into care, and she would come in by herself before going to visit him in the nursing home. Our little cafe was part of her life; an anchor in the storm for her. I honestly contemplated keeping the business running just for her.

I came to realise that the work of the cafe was complete. We had built up a good little business with a healthy reputation, but the season was over. We put the business on the market and waited for a buyer. I had started university and was fumbling my way through unfamiliar territory. The first semester was brutal. Naively, I had enrolled full-time with no clue as to how gruelling this new world of study would be. Thankfully, I was a distance education student, so all my learning was online. I had no interest in university life and making new friends. I was here to study and to get my magic piece of paper that would allow me to venture into the uncharted territory of a brand-new work life.

As I had dropped out of school, essay writing and research writing was the equivalent to understanding Spanish; I had no idea what I was doing! When the results came back for my first semester it was the reality check I needed. I failed two out of the four units. I was conflicted between feeling proud and excited about passing two units while simultaneously embarrassed and disappointed for failing the other two. I wanted to quit. I was feeling sorry for myself as my ego had been royally kicked. Failing confirmed that I was stupid and not fit for the academic world. However, passing meant that the ability to succeed existed. I just needed to make some changes and be humble.

The comparison went around and around in my head.

"Other people don't struggle with ..."

"Other people manage working full time and study full time..."

"Other people can cram and get high grades..."

"It's easy for so many other people..."

Ah, the dialogue of an immature woman. Making excuses is always a sign of pride but thankfully I decided to get over myself and do two things. One, change to part time study for at least one year, or at least until I became more competent at this new skill I was acquiring called study. And two, I was going to ask for help. I approached one of my closest friends, Sal, who had served her time at university and had a more academic brain than I did. She understood the requirements of university and the techniques needed for academic writing. She was my saving grace! From then on Sal received late night phone calls from me. Being sleep deprived and confused by my wordsmithing, Sal would patiently and calmly reassure me that either I was on the right track or she would redirect me, helping me to understand what I was supposed to focus on. Sal read through every assignment for me, teaching me how to structure my writing, how to properly back up my writing with evidence, and how to stay on topic and to acknowledge that not every big idea is relevant!

As I'd left school at the end of year ten, I was behind with reading and writing. I really did not understand all the rules of grammar. Sal would constantly break down laughing while reading my assignments as I battled with knowing when to use being or been, and entire paragraphs were one sentence.

"But that's how I talk! I don't take breaths when I'm talking, so why do I need to break down my writing?" was my objection.

I had never properly mastered these skills so there was a lot of learning to be done. Changing my expectation of university from producing perfection to accepting that this was a time of learning on many levels, was the key to forging on. Learning a skill positions you to accept that if you are not competent in a particular area, you have the ability to develop yourself in that area. It has nothing to do with my character, although my character is exposed in the way I respond. This wasn't a reflection on my academic ability; it revealed the areas that were weak and needed improving. I would read over an essay with Sal and laugh with her as we tried to decode sections of writing. Eventually we got there, and I started to enjoy writing, in particular research writing. I confess that referencing still challenges me and I really don't understand how to properly reference.

In 2014 I was thirty-two years old when we sold Tall Poppy Cafe. It was such a bittersweet feeling. Seven years ago, I had felt so strongly that opening this little cafe was a step of faith and believed that God had big plans for two young women in their early twenties. What we built wasn't perfect and our working relationship was hard at times, but we decided to be obedient to the Lord by saying yes to the dream, and yes to the possibility that God could touch our community through this business. Through countless cups of coffee and tons of love that was poured out from myself and our team, I know without a doubt that Tall Poppy had served its purpose for that time. I had fought for my life during those years and through the pain I found a way forward that only God could lead me through. The pressure of the whole journey had not broken me but had started the process of reforming me.

During this year of selling the business I also came off medication which I had been taking for twelve years for anxiety and depression. This was nothing short of a miracle. There was still pressure around my life; pressure never went away. Nonetheless, little by little I was learning to look beyond the natural chaos that we live in and focus on God's voice and what He was putting in front of me. Instead of trying to understand myself though my limited thinking I was establishing my identity in who God was.

The day I knew I was free from depression was like a private surprise party. Sounds weird I know. I was simply driving down a familiar road, a road that usually flicked a switch inside of me and suicidal thoughts would come flooding into my mind. This time as I was driving, I became intensely aware that there was no urge, no thought, no idea of suicide. The battle was over! Depression was officially evicted! This moment gave me intense hope and faith that through God's love and grace our minds can be reset and restored to a place of peace and soundness. This miracle is for anyone! I need to remind you that there is a significant difference between feeling low and feeling sad, to experiencing depression. Feeling sad or low, even extreme versions of these feelings, are normal given the right circumstances. Depression is a force that has one goal - to destroy the person it is attached to. It is a type of cancer that feeds off darkness. When someone is fighting depression, they are fighting hell.

As I write, I am now ten years free from medication and free from depression. I am twenty years on from when the first doctor told me that medication might be a permanent part of my life. I am thirty-two years on from when the displacing thoughts of suicide and gender confusion first entered my mind.

"Freedom must be fought for, protected, and handed on to the next generation for them to do the same." (Ronald Reagan, 1982).

The freedom that I have won in my life is not something that should ever be taken for granted. Too many people believe that they are entitled to good mental health and don't realise the battle required to not only free your mind from darkness but to also keep guarding your heart and your mind from future invasions. The battle of the heart and mind that God led me through during those years was not won simply for me to feel comfortable and have an easy life. I assure you that this is not the case. The battle equipped me to stay free and walk with others as they take on their own war zone within themselves. I do not accept that poor mental health and our current high suicide rates are normal. They are common but not normal, and I want nothing more than to fight for this next generation as they face the challenges set before them.

The freedom that I have found in my mind started with the healing of my heart. My mind is renewed because of the Spirit of God gaining access to me, and through relationships with people who also have a strong faith in God who have already won the battle of the mind. Our culture preaches that independence is the answer to freedom and that following your feelings will lead to fulfilment. What delusional lies! We are built for relationships; we are created to walk in unity.

A hand is a very important part of the human body; without it, life would be very challenging. However, if you cut the hand off, all it is now is a home for maggots. The hand needs the life of the body to fulfil its purpose. If the hand is injured, the rest of the body works to heal the it. If the body does not respond like this, but instead leaves the hand isolated, not only would the hand suffer more but it would put the rest of the body at risk. It's in the best interest of the human body that every area works and functions to its full ability.

In John 13:34 Jesus commands us to love one another. It's not a suggestion, it is a requirement. To love ensures healing. The command to love is for the ones we see as friends as well as for our enemies. That does not mean we allow people to mistreat us but rather it's a way for us to resist bitterness and entertaining any desire to take revenge. How? By giving God the grievance of our heart again and again until we are free. Over time I have felt the pain not only from my own actions but from those of others who have hurt me. Sometimes the pain is unbearable, and thoughts of hatred may even be justified. However, justifying my position is like setting a snare for myself. Loving one another is not about loving someone out of our own limited ability. Nor is it about ignoring the pain. Rather, we bring the pain to God and allow Him, who is love, to love that person for us.

I had to learn how to 'connect to the body.' I had to work hard to build healthy relationships to heal from the wounds of the past, as well as upgrade my thinking. God connected me to an inspiring church, a body of people that, despite their imperfections, were dedicated to seeking God first. We are all following someone, but who are the people following that we are following, and where are they headed?

Freedom is gained through discipline and dedication. It is neither a right nor an entitlement. I am not a victim of my past. I am not hard done by the circumstances I grew up in. I thank God every day for my family and my upbringing. God gave me parents who, despite their upbringing, were determined to build something new for themselves and their young family. I have siblings who have shown me resilience and determination. How blessed I am to have had all these characteristics built into me. But unless I looked at things from my new position, which is in Christ Jesus, then I am more than certain I would have become overwhelmed by the shadows that tried to cover up the God-given life inside of me.

Chapter 18

Understanding Comes After Commitment

Truly, we want to be without pain and shame, so we do all we can to protect ourselves, avoiding the reality of our position and what is inside each of us. We hide, like in Genesis chapter 3. Adam followed Eve's suggestion to obtain life outside of God. As soon as they committed themselves to eating from the tree of knowledge, separation from God immediately took place. They chose to sustain themselves rather than finding life with their Creator. Adam hid from God, knowing that he had disobeyed Him and was now seeing the world around him without God's presence. But what is God's response to a shameful Adam? God calls out to Adam. His will is to restore and make whole. God makes Himself known to Adam, but when confronted by God, Adam blames God for his own decision.

In essence Adam claimed that God's own creation had caused him to sin and made him want more than what he had been given - "*The woman you gave me made me...*" Genesis 3:12). The understanding of what it meant to be "equal with God" came after Adam committed to disobeying God. God, who provides, could no longer provide for him. God, who protects, could no longer protect him. God, who sustains life, was excluded. Death was introduced and with it, pain and suffering and a constant battle to come back into right relationship with God.

God's heart never changes toward the one whom He loves. Jesus was the perfect sacrifice that had to be made for reconciliation between us and God. When we ask, God responds. I knew I had to ask God to forgive me. Now, I hadn't broken the law or done anything particularly regrettable, but my heart was full of lies that I had not only allowed in, but I had fed those lies. My heart needed to be healed from my thinking. Repentance is not about shaming, it's about renewing. Therefore, asking God to forgive me for what I had been thinking and believing allowed God to rebuild and restore me to what He had always intended.

Romans 8:1 was becoming a reality, a lived revelation. Condemnation was fading as I was retraining myself to come into His presence and live according to His Spirit.

We really have no choice. Our arrogance, our pain, and our shame keep us searching for freedom outside of God and His ways. Remove God and you remove life. Working is not the way to achieve God's approval.

Chapter 19

So, Who Am I?

I am a woman who sees no limitation to what God can do. My confidence comes not from my skills and abilities, as they will always be limited in some way. No, my confidence comes more and more from God as He is well able. He is well able to heal the brokenhearted (Luke 4:18). He loves me and has never given up on me (Hebrews 4:16). My God is a champion, and He champions those He loves. He repositions us - from lost and hopeless to standing with confidence by His side (Psalm 40:2).

I am a woman who intensely loves those who are wounded and battling, as God has shown His love for me. This love is so passionate that He gave His Son as the only worthy sacrifice for my redemption. That little chubby girl, growing up in a broken family, living in a town that no one had heard of. That little girl who believed that suicide was her future and that her sense of belonging was somehow intertwined with her gender. That little girl was nothing special or outstanding to any onlooker, but to God, Who created her, she was a jewel in His crown (Zechariah 9:16).

I am a woman who finds joy in times of darkness and is determined to celebrate what God has done. I look around and see so many people who have had victories and overcome their battles

(Philippians 4:4). Joy is refreshing and is a weapon in pursuing freedom.

I am a woman free from condemnation (Romans 8:1). The Spirit of God is a spirit of liberty and renews our mind as we humble ourselves and allow God to have His way in us. His will is for us to be united with Him (Romans 8:6).

I am a woman who values the friends and family around me. Together we grow and find our purpose and belonging in God. (1 Corinthians 12:13.)

The question of "who am I?" is an age-old question, and in our modern world we are deceived into believing that who we are is packaged neatly in our career, our status, our acceptance within social settings, our gender, our cash flow, our children, and so many other things. We live in a country where we have the biggest houses, the lowest unemployment figures, and more opportunities than ever before, but we, as a people, are drowning in depression and anxiety. Eighty percent of people in our nation are either on prescription medication or they self-medicate. We are lost. We are disconnected from the God who gives life and whose love is greater than any achievement we could ever gain. The love of God is absent in our modern world, and we are paying a great price for it.

Today, I am who I am because I found myself when I found God and allowed Him to reveal Himself to me. I know who I am because I know the great I AM.

Chapter 20

Did I Finish University?

Six years after that leap of faith into the academic world, I completed a bachelor's degree and then went on to finish a Master of Social Work. Academics is still not a strength of mine, but I'm no longer intimidated by it. The vision of helping other people overcome their limitations motivated me to obey what I believed was the next step for me. I have grown up and gotten over myself in so many ways because of university and the pressure that comes with it.

Jill and David Murphy, at my graduation, 2020

When you fail, you discover that you're made of 'the good, the bad, and the ugly'. Failure gives you opportunity after opportunity to become stronger and more accurate with your vision. True failure is giving up and giving in.

I am continually amazed at the life I live. Every day, I thank God for what He has given me, which is new life. The reality of the life I could have lived has made me understand what the fear of God is. Without Him, hell has free range over your life and over your thinking. In Him, we are set free from a limiting, long-suffering life.

I don't fear what God can do; I fear what life is like without Him.

I have been brought to my knees many times by the challenges and heartache that have come in recent years, but my anchor is in my understanding of who God is. I no longer get tossed around by the chaos of the storm but allow the Holy Spirit to inhabit my heart and my thoughts so that I can see things from God's presence rather than my fearful perspective.

My expectations for the future keep expanding! Taking risks is part of a fulfilling adventure. If I could give one piece of advice, it would be this - take risks and realise that comfort is a trap; I would rather have people see me fail and witness a marvellous recovery, which demonstrates God's glory. I will never deny the continual battle at times to beat off old thinking. Unhealthy thoughts are like a professional burglar. They are familiar with their surroundings; they know the entry points and the most vulnerable times to gain access. To evict these burglars, having a sense of purpose is a strong driving force, as well as diving deeper into God's Word and maintaining life-giving friendships that surround me.

My passion for helping young people is driven by the hope that listening to their heartache and loving them regardless of their behaviours and actions, while speaking life into them, can potentially allow them access to the same life-giving freedom I have experienced.

I have learned that as parents, it is a privilege to be stewards of a child's life. If parents are not having real talks with their children, this is what will happen: when they begin to go through their challenges and inner struggles, they may be attracted to the 'realness' of influences on the Gram, on TikTok, or YouTube (social media). The people on these forms of media are called influencers for a reason. Children are looking for authenticity, and when they are feeling broken, they will look for someone they can trust who displays the answer to their brokenness; they will look for someone who is 'real'. Have conversations with your children, but more than that, listen to what their hearts are saying. Show them who should influence them, connect them with the body, which is the wider community/family, so that they can find life and purpose.

As a therapist working with teenagers now, I have regular conversations with parents explaining that their child craves connection with their parents. Of course, there is a place for seeking counsel, and teenagers will naturally seek others for guidance at some stage, and this should be encouraged! Parents are key to these healthy connections. As a Christian, I sometimes wonder if the current mental health crisis is a reflection of our failure to understand what God says about many of the issues our youth are up against. Have we misinterpreted what blessing is and now seek financial freedom over seeking first the kingdom of God?

Having people speak God's word into my heart and teach me how to dig deep into the word of God myself, is what delivered me from the belief that my life was not worth living. Asking God to forgive me for allowing these thoughts to narrate my life also set me free. "But you were just a child when these thoughts entered your mind!" Yes, but as an adult, I saw those thoughts as my identity and part of who I was. God needed me to reject those patterns of thought so that I could take on His way of thinking, His way of seeing, and His way of loving.

Romans 7:18 (ESV), *For I have the desire to do what is right, but not the ability to carry it out.*

Many people over the years have spoken life into me, which has been like breath into the dry bones within me. The people closest to me were not moved or shocked by the rawness or the pain; they could see God's potential within me. This is now how I try and see every young person I spend time with – each one lovingly created by God.

Chapter 21

Can These Dry Bones Live?

Thank you, dear reader! May God reveal Himself to you, that you would know of His goodness and graciousness. His love has already overcome every issue of darkness, and now we are on the journey of reconciling with the truth of His love and goodness at work in our lives.

A final Scripture that captured my attention and my imagination at the very beginning of my journey with God:

> Ezekiel 37:1-6 (NIV), *The hand of the Lord was on me, and he brought me out by the Spirit of the Lord and set me in the middle of a valley; it was full of bones. He led me back and forth among them, and I saw a great many bones on the floor of the valley, bones that were very dry. He asked me, "Son of man, can these bones live?"*
> *I said, "Sovereign Lord, you alone know."*
> *Then he said to me, "Prophesy to these bones and say to them, 'Dry bones, hear the word of the Lord! This is what the Sovereign Lord says to these bones: I will make breath enter you, and you will come to life. I will attach tendons to you and make flesh come upon you and cover you with skin; I will put breath in you, and you will come to life. Then you will know that I am the Lord."*

This scripture ignited a passion in me that captivated my whole being. My mind, my heart, and the possibility of God's greatness and His love for us engulfed my heart. Can these dry bones live? This was the question that spoke to me personally and revealed to me my purpose. Could God breathe life into an already dead-end soul? Could God cause me to be raised to life by His Spirit? And could God breathe life into the forgotten people? The destitute lives of a generation living in chaos and delusion? The answer is yes. Yes, He is willing and able. His love goes beyond our understanding, and His heart's desire is for us to be restored into His presence - through Jesus and His life of sacrifice, by His obedience, by His love for us through His heavenly Father. Jesus has enabled us to be reconciled to our God, our Father, our Creator. God's love is for us to be restored to life.

A prayer of reconciliation between you and our great God:

"Father God, I love you. I believe in you. I need you.
I'm sorry for my sins. Sorry about the way I've lived.
Sorry for shutting You out.
I want You in my life, I surrender, I yield,
I receive Jesus as my Saviour and my Lord;
I believe He died for me. He rose from the dead. He's alive today.
Come into me. Take me just the way I am.
Now make me everything You want me to be.
I believe I'm saved through Jesus Christ.
Amen."

Acknowledgments

My heartfelt thanks to my family. They are all champions who have impacted me and inspired me to keep moving forward. My mother and father set the example of risk-taking and perseverance. My siblings set the standard that victimhood was not an option. Joy is one of the greatest tools for getting on with it. I am forever thankful for the family I have; my brother and sister are still two of my most cherished and favourite people in the world - they too never gave up on our family and continue to show a great deal of gratitude for what we were given.

My pastors, Brian and Lynne; thank God you chose a life of obedience to God. The joy that you bring to others and I could not be more grateful for the endless encouragement through countless conversations and moments we spent together. You have both championed me through every peak and every trough. You both possess a level of humility, a passion for others, and a desire for God that has inspired me from the very beginning. Your walk with God has not been easy, but it has made a way for those like me. Thank you for the sacrifices you have made and for being determined to win the battles that you have had to fight. Giving up is never the solution; giving over to God has become the only way.

To Val Hall, the super nanny of all super nannies! Even now, at age eighty-eight, the energy and passion you have for others runs rings around most twenty-year-olds. Age is a state of mind, and watching you live your life I see that you really can get younger as you get older. Your boldness to share your love for

God set things in motion for me. Even more inspiring is that you have never wavered, regardless of what has been thrown at you; you have only been strengthened in your faith! Ageing doesn't look scary or depressing when I look at you; so, I will keep watching and be inspired by you as you dance across the finish line.

To Yvonne and Michael, taking a teen girl into an already lively house was a sacrifice that I am forever grateful for. Patience and kindness are qualities you both possess. Your love for others is infectious, and the creativity and resourcefulness you both harness make family life incredibly exciting. You took me in as one of your own, and for this I thank God.

My dear friends, you know who you are. My love for you all is so incredibly deep. I will fight for you as you have fought for me in prayer and friendship. You have all, in some way, been a light in a dark place. How grateful I am to have you all in my life!

www.ingramcontent.com/pod-product-compliance
Lightning Source LLC
Chambersburg PA
CBHW061209070526
44583CB00025B/3174